PRAYING
DANGEROUSLY

PRAYING
DANGEROUSLY

Daring Prayers for Meaningful Faith

Gary Holloway

LEAFWOOD

PRAYING DANGEROUSLY:
Daring Prayers for Meaningful Faith

L E A F W O O D
P U B L I S H E R S

ISBN 978-0-89112-675-1
LCCN 2010017259

Printed in the United States of America

LIBRARY OF CONGRESS CATALOGING-IN-PUBLICATION DATA
Holloway, Gary, 1956-
Praying dangerously : daring prayers for meaningful faith / Gary Holloway.
    p. cm.
ISBN 978-0-89112-675-1
1. Bible--Prayers. I. Title.
BS680.P64H65 2010
248.3'2--dc22
                                                            2010017259

Cover design by Marc Whitaker
Interior text design by Sandy Armstrong

Leafwood Publishers
1626 Campus Court
Abilene, Texas 79601
1-877-816-4455 toll free

For current information about all Leafwood titles, visit our Web site:
www.leafwoodpublishers.com

10 11 12 13 14 15 / 7 6 5 4 3 2 1

To JoAnn Harwell
and Art and Lonnie Peddle,
people of prayer

CONTENTS

PART FIVE

Praying with Early Christians in Acts and the Letters

INTRODUCTION

You're hurdling down a rain-swept road at fifty miles an hour. Sideways. Your car is completely out of control and the car stalled in your lane grows closer with each passing second. Time seems to stand still as you realize you will crash. What do you do? Even if you've never been to church and aren't sure you believe in God, in those few long out-of-control seconds, you pray. You pray because you are in danger.

Everybody prays. Well, most everybody. According to a recent poll, less than 50% of Americans belong to a church, fewer attend regularly, but over 90% pray. One might think prayer is a natural, universally human phenomenon. If prayer comes naturally, then why should we have to learn to pray?

There is prayer and there is biblical prayer, just as there is worship and biblical worship. Human beings are incurably religious: they have been known to worship trees, idols, money, success, and happiness. Not all worship is to the one true God. Not all prayer is prayer to him. Even we who worship that one God must worship in ways that please him. We tend to pray to whatever "god" can save us from our immediate danger.

But the Bible shows us another way of prayer. We pray to a living God who might save us from danger, but who himself *is* dangerous. Why? Because he is a God we cannot fathom. A God we cannot control. We must learn that extremely risky prayer that Jesus learned to pray: "May God's will, not mine be done."

So how does one learn to pray such dangerous prayers? We learn from people of faith. For many of us it was faithful parents who first taught us to pray. I still fondly recall those childhood lessons: folding the hands together, bowing the head, and saying "God is great, God is good . . ." or "Now I lay me down to sleep." I grew beyond those childhood prayers and learned to pray from other church members—Peggy

Cofield, who taught me in Sunday school, Roger McKenzie, our first preacher, and countless others whose names I have forgotten who taught me how to bow before God and humbly commune with him. I continue to learn how to pray from my family and from my church.

But it is not enough to pray the way we have always been taught. That's what some thought about 2000 years ago. They had prayed all their lives. They thought they knew how. Until they met the young rabbi from Nazareth. Then they saw a depth of prayer they had never experienced before. They heard someone who risked everything in prayer. So they asked him, "Lord, teach us to pray."

But we cannot fully understand Christ's teachings on prayer without a grasp of prayer in the Old Testament. The Lord's Prayer is his answer to his disciples' request for instruction in prayer. Yet how many phrases in that most famous of prayers would have been foreign to the disciples without their prior heritage of prayer found in the Old Testament? "Father," "heaven," "holy," "kingdom," "forgiveness," and "temptation" were all themes of Old Testament prayer before Jesus ever spoke these words.

Certainly we should model our prayer lives after Jesus and the early disciples, but when Jesus taught them to pray, he did not have to start from scratch. He spoke to people with a rich heritage of prayer to their heavenly Father. We also can learn to pray from these faithful ones. We can learn as Jesus himself learned to pray—by praying with God's people in the Bible.

The Old Testament holds great value for Christian prayer. In these pages you will rediscover and reclaim that heritage. Here we meet men and women who turned to God in joy and sorrow, triumph and defeat, faithfulness and sin. By seeing how they prayed, we too can learn to bow before our God in all the circumstances of life.

This book will first lead you through the prayers of the Old Testament section by section—Pentateuch, Historical Books, Poetical Books, and Prophets. In each section we will look at the prayers thematically. There we will find that we pray the same kinds of prayers that God's people prayed long ago.

These are not merely ancient prayers in an ancient culture to an ancient God. They are living prayers to a living God. When we bow before the Father and cry out to him, we join countless others in the past who have found him faithful. He hears! He speaks! He acts!

His greatest act was to become one of us. One above all is our teacher on prayer.

It is Jesus who answers his disciples' request, "Lord, teach us to pray."

One way Jesus teaches us to pray is through the New Testament. Having looked at Old Testament prayer, this book then examines what the New Testament says about prayer. Not every passage that mentions prayer is included, but every major prayer text is here. These passages are organized under headings, but I have resisted the temptation to systematize these teachings too much. Instead, I follow the basic order of the New Testament.

This book is intended to change your life. It is meant to force you to read what the Bible says on prayer. Not only to read, but to reflect. Not only to reflect, but to pray. And if you pray, your life will be changed. You can read this book in various ways. You may read it privately, with another Christian, in a small group Bible study, or in a class at church. However you read it, my prayer is that this book will help you and your church rediscover the habit of prayer and to learn what Jesus and the early church knew: true power comes only through prayer. Remember, the first disciples asked Jesus, "Lord, teach us to pray." He still teaches, if we will learn.

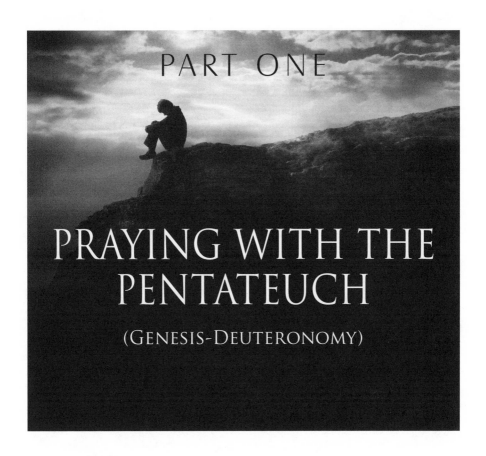

PART ONE

PRAYING WITH THE PENTATEUCH

(Genesis-Deuteronomy)

CHAPTER 1

"They Bowed before the Lord"
Prayer as Fear and Trembling

"Then the man bowed down and worshipped the Lord."

Genesis 24:26

Adam and Eve, Cain and Abel, Noah, Abraham, Sarah, Isaac, Joseph, Moses, Miriam, and Aaron. We remember their stories. We see in our mind's eye the garden, the well, the prison, and the mountain where each had an encounter with the Almighty. These are the Bible stories of our youth. In these first five books of the Bible, we learned of faith and sin, of cowardice and heroism, of victory and defeat.

Strangely enough, we read relatively little on prayer in these books. This may surprise us. After all, we usually call these books the books of Law. "Law" is an unfortunate translation of the Hebrew word "Torah." A better translation would be "instruction." In these biblical books we have not a list of laws, but God's instruction to his people, inviting them to live in covenant with him.

It is quite surprising, then, to find that these books have no specific instructions or laws on prayer. God tells his people what to eat, how to dress, how to treat diseases, and how to sacrifice, but nowhere does he tell them directly how to pray. Is prayer unimportant to God? Of course not. Instead, God's instruction on prayer in the first five books of the Bible is not found in rules or laws, but in examples. He shows us how to pray in those familiar stories of Abraham, Moses, and the Israelites at prayer.

Prayer is taught not by rules, or lists, or books on prayer. Prayer is taught by praying. Praying like Jesus and the apostles. Like Abraham, Moses, and Israel. It's almost as if the Bible begins with a warning about prayer: do not confuse learning *about* prayer with learning to pray. It is only by seeing prayer "live" in the personal struggles of the faithful that we learn how to pray. By praying like them, our prayer life is shaped into the image God wants. Let us look at these faithful ones to see how their prayer lives can shape ours.

Abraham: Face Down Before God

The first example of prayer in the Old Testament does not even use the word "prayer," but refers rather to bowing before God in reverence and gratitude:

When Abram was ninety-nine years old, the Lord appeared to him and said, "I am God Almighty; walk before me and be blameless. I will confirm my covenant between me and you and will greatly increase your numbers."

Abram fell face down, and God said to him, "As for me, this is my covenant with you: You will be the father of many nations. No longer will you be called Abram; your name will be Abraham, for I have made you the father of many nations. I will make you very fruitful; I will make nations of you, and kings will come from you. I will establish my covenant as an everlasting covenant between me and you and your descendants after you for the generations to come, to be your God and the God of your descendants after you. The whole land of Canaan, where you are now an alien, I will give as an everlasting possession to you and your descendants after you; and I will be their God." (Genesis 17:1-8)

Here the initiative is wholly with God. He appears to Abraham. He offers to bless him. He makes the covenant. Abraham's reaction to the appearance of such a gracious God is the same as ours should be: he falls on his face in thankfulness and respect.

Of course, if I tell you today that someone "fell face down," it paints quite a different picture than the biblical one. Abraham is not performing a pratfall, but rather is recognizing the full authority of God. Falling on one's face, stretched out face downward on the ground, was the proper way in the ancient world to show subservience to a king. If earthly rulers were greeted in this way, then how much more should we fall prostrate before the King of all creation?

But falling face down before others does not come naturally to contemporary Americans. We strongly believe that all persons are equal. The sight of someone prostrating himself before an foreign despot may be not merely strange, but even offensive to us. In a democracy, such a custom is ancient and barbarous.

Yet if we are not careful, our attitude of equality, of being as good as the next fellow no matter how high and mighty he or she is, can carry over to our relationship with God. No one would claim equality with God, but we may forget how utterly unlike us God really is. Creator, all-powerful ruler of the universe, completely Holy God is he. We do not control this God. He is a dangerous God. In his presence our only proper attitude is to grovel face down as unworthy servants.

Abraham falls face down, not just out of reverence and fear, but out of gratitude. The good news for Abraham (and for us) is that this all-powerful, all-holy God has by his grace chosen to make covenant with us. We bow in amazement at the blessings he has in store for us, blessings we do not deserve.

By bowing before God we recognize the distance between him and us. Ironically, it is while we face the ground before him that we also realize our intimacy with him. In this posture of humility and gratitude, we can approach him boldly. While he is on his face, Abraham can even question the promises of God:

> God also said to Abraham, "As for Sarai your wife, you are no longer to call her Sarai; her name shall be Sarah. I will bless her and will surely give you a son by her. I will bless her so that she will be the mother of nations; kings will come from her."
>
> Abraham fell face down; he laughed and said to himself, "Will a son be born to a man a hundred years old? Will Sarah bear a child at the age of ninety?" And Abraham said to God, "If only Ishmael might live under your blessing!" (Genesis 17:15-17)

How can Abraham laugh at God? What kind of laugh is this? A laugh of joy or a laugh of incredulity? It appears to be the latter. Abraham can hardly believe that he and Sarah will have a child at their age. He even has an alternate plan, "Oh, that Ishmael might live in your sight!" But God answers, "No, but your wife Sarah shall bear you a son."

Abraham laughs. Later, when Sarah overhears the promise that she will have a son, she too laughs. God gets angry with her, asking, "Why did Sarah laugh?" and "Is anything too hard for the Lord?" (Genesis 18:13-14). Why is God angry at Sarah's laugh, but not at Abraham's? I'm not sure, but perhaps it has something to do with their attitudes and even their posture before God.

How can Abraham risk laughing at God? Why doesn't the Almighty zap him? Because he laughs from a position of reverence and thankfulness. He falls on his face. In the intimacy of prayer we also can be honest with God. We can express our doubts and, yes, even laugh at his promises. But only if we do so while on our faces, acknowledging that he is God and we are not.

Have you ever been in Abraham's shoes? Has the news from God ever been so good yet so fantastic that you laughed in disbelief? Some of us have. We've wanted a child for so long, but have been told we can't have children. Until that wonderful day when the doctor said, "I don't understand it, but you're pregnant." We laugh. Out of relief, joy, and disbelief we laugh. Or we've been told the cancer is terminal. No hope. Then at our next check-up the tumor is gone. Disappeared without a trace. We think it a bad joke. We laugh. But it's true. Too good to be, but true.

Abraham laughed. Sometimes when God surprises us, we laugh too. We do not laugh to ridicule God, but we laugh from our knees in awe of the God who accomplishes what seems impossible, even ridiculous to us.

Abraham's Servant: Bowing and Worshipping

Abraham's servant also bows his head in gratitude before God. Abraham sends him back to the home country to find a wife for Isaac. He travels far, arrives at Nahor, and stops at the village well. There he prays and makes God a proposition: "Let the girl that offers me a drink be the one you have appointed for Isaac." Sure enough, Rebekah comes, offers him and his camels drink, and runs home to prepare a place for him to stay. The servant is overwhelmed with this immediate answer to prayer. "Then the man bowed down and worshipped the Lord, saying, 'Praise be to the Lord, the God of my master Abraham, who has not abandoned his kindness and faithfulness to my master. As for me, the Lord has led me on the journey to the house of my master's relatives'" (Genesis 24:26-27).

There is still one obstacle in the way of the servant: will Rebekah's father Bethuel permit her to marry Isaac? When the servant tells the story of his prayer, Bethuel and his son Laban say, "This is from the Lord; we cannot say one way or the other. Here is Rebekah; take her and go, and let her become the wife of your master's son, as the Lord directed" (Genesis 24:50-51). When the servant hears this, he again bows himself to the ground before the Lord (Genesis 24:52).

At first this story may confuse us about prayer. Are we to assume that we can set up hypothetical situations for God and he will always come through with what we ask? Such is a dangerous view of prayer for it borders on making God our slave instead of our Master. We must remember that the servant asked with a bowed head and received with a grateful heart. God will answer our prayers, but only when we pray in the attitude of worship.

This case is also unusual because the answer comes with no action on the part of the servant. All he does is pray and wait for God to act. Sometimes God does answer prayer this way, but we should not expect he does every time. Sometimes he answers by working through our own efforts.

God still answers our search for the right bride or husband, or the right job or the right home. His answers to us might be less immediate and dramatic than to Abraham's servant. They might not be what we want to hear. They will be given on God's timetable, not ours. I believe with all my heart that God heard my frequent prayer years ago to give me a wife who would keep me close to him. My wife Deb is all I asked for and more, the greatest blessing of my life. But I didn't test God in prayer, "Lord, let the next woman in green passing through the door be the one I should marry." Perhaps there are times when we can do this with God. Abraham's servant did. But even then we must do it with bowed heads and worshipful hearts, praying that his will, not ours, be done.

The Israelites: Faith and Worship

How do we know God really cares for us? Because the Bible says so! Yes, but what if we still find it hard to believe? We can rely on how God has blessed us in the past. But what if we've known nothing but bad times for years on end? What if God is hiding his face from us? If we cannot see his blessings, how do we know he cares?

It may happen in illness. How can God let me suffer so? It may be loss of a loved one. How could God take her away from me when he knows how lost I am without her? It may be when unemployment and poverty strike us through no fault of our own. Where is God? Why has he left me? Does he care?

These are the questions the Israelites asked while slaves in Egypt. Why had the God of their fathers, the God of Abraham, Isaac, and Jacob, abandoned them? Had he not promised an eternal covenant to them? How could he let his people suffer? In the midst of such questions, mired in despair, we are tempted to turn our back on God since it appears he turned his back on us. Israel does not do this. They cry out to God in their pain. They dare to pray to God even when it seems he is not listening.

And God hears them! He calls Moses at the burning bush and sends him to deliver Israel. But Moses had one overriding fear: "What if they do not believe me or listen to me and say, 'The Lord did not appear to you'?" (Exodus 4:1). For those who have been down so long, the good news of deliverance is hard to believe. So God gives Moses miraculous signs to convince the Israelites that God is with them.

As he arrives in Egypt, the question remains: will the people of Israel accept his mission as being from God? He makes his case before Israel's elders:

> Moses and Aaron brought together all the elders of the Israelites, and Aaron told them everything the Lord had said to Moses. He also performed the signs before the people, and they believed. And when they heard that the Lord was concerned about them and had seen their misery, they bowed down and worshipped. (Exodus 4:29-31)

God cares! He has not abandoned us. He is here to deliver us, to save us from the death of slavery. What can we do in the face of God's faithful love except bow in humble gratitude?

Few face literal slavery today, but many of us face our own personal masters: depression, despair, temptations we can't quite overcome, people who dog our step and make life miserable, and the list goes on. We feel forgotten by God. But then the news comes: he has heard our cries. He has seen our misery. He cares. He brings strength and relief. We bow and worship.

No matter how bad things get, we must never stop praying, never stop crying out to God in our misery. We may not think he hears us, but we must not stop. He does. He will deliver us from evil in his own good time. He gives strength for whatever faces us. We must never stop asking him and never stop thanking him for his gracious gifts. This is the essence of prayer.

In the midst of pain and even in the routines of life, we need reminders of how God has delivered us in the past, reminders to thank him and to continue to trust his grace. As God delivers the Israelites from Egypt, he gives them a reminder of his love: the Passover meal. The meal is not just for those in Egypt, but for generations to come who were never slaves and may be tempted to forget the power and love of their God:

> Obey these instructions as a lasting ordinance for you and your descendants. When you enter the land the Lord will give you as he promised, observe this ceremony. And when your children ask you, "What does this ceremony mean to you?" then tell them, "It is the Passover sacrifice to the Lord, who passed over the houses of the Israelites in Egypt and spared our homes when he struck down the Egyptians." Then the people bowed down and worshipped. (Exodus 12:24-28)

Christians too have been given ceremonies and ordinances to remind us of our deliverance through Christ. Chief among these is the Lord's Supper. Unfortunately in our society, "ceremony" and "ritual" have become bad words. If we do the same things in worship each Sunday, we soon grow tired of the same old rituals and ceremonies. We long for something new and exciting.

How different was Israel's reaction to the Passover. When told that this ceremony should be practiced throughout their generations, the Israelites bow and worship God. No doubt their prayer was one of thanks for God freeing them from slavery, but it also was thanks for the Passover as a reminder of his love.

In the same way, we should be thankful, not critical, of the ceremonies God gives us as reminders. If we do not find prayer, hymns, Scripture reading, and the Lord's Supper "meaningful," we need to ask the question children ask at the Passover, "What do these things mean?" At Passover, this is an opportunity for telling the story of the Exodus: "We were slaves in Egypt and the Lord delivered us with a mighty hand." We too need to rehearse our story: we were slaves to sin and God delivered us by the blood of his Son. This is the heart of our worship ceremonies. For this we bow and worship God.

The Israelites, however, were no better than we. In spite of these reminders of God's care, when times got tough they complained and turned against him. In the desert, when water grew scarce, they asked Moses and Aaron, "Why did you bring us up out of Egypt to this terrible place? It has no grain or figs, grapevines or pomegranates. And there is no water to drink" (Numbers 20:5).

Moses and Aaron go to the Tent of Meeting to ask God for water. They go in fear for the people, for they have complained against God. They fall face down before God, his glory appears, and he tells them how he will send water.

This is the last example in the Pentateuch of falling down or bowing before the Lord. Here we are reminded that one bows in reverence, in gratitude, but also in repentance. Moses and Aaron are requesting help from God, but help for a stubborn, complaining people. We too are often stubborn and complaining. When we realize we are, we must bow in shame before the God who is good enough to bless us, stubborn and complaining as we are.

Should We Bow?

Abraham, his servant, Aaron, Moses, and all Israel bowed face down before God. Should we?

The truth is, I've never seen a Christian bow face down before God. We don't at church. There's not enough room in the aisles. We pray sitting or standing or (rarely) kneeling. In restaurants, I've seen Christians bow their heads, but never their whole bodies. Imagine the fuss that would make.

So should we bow, throw ourselves face down, in prayer? Not in restaurants, surely, for to do so would tempt us too much to pray to be seen by others, a practice Jesus condemns. Probably not yet in church worship, just because it would be too novel a practice for most churches. We might be tempted to think it "exciting" and "neat" and forget the real purpose of bowing down: to show reverence to God.

In our own private place of prayer, we should at times fall face down before our God. To do so recognizes his power, his holiness, and his love. We fall in humility, in reverence, and in gratitude. What we can learn from these ancient people of faith is not some new prayer posture, but the attitude we must have in prayer no matter what our posture. If our bodies sit or stand or kneel, inwardly we are bowing, face to the ground, before the Almighty Ruler of the creation.

Questions for Further Discussion

1. Does it make any difference if we bow or kneel or stand for prayer? What does our bodily posture communicate when we pray? Are some postures more spiritual than others?

2. Should we dare to ask God for signs of his will, as Abraham's servant did? Why or why not?

3. Why does God sometimes take so long to answer our prayers? What should our attitude be as we wait for an answer?

4. How do we keep church rituals from becoming meaningless? What connection is there between those ceremonies and prayer?

5. What seems to be the attitude of Abraham, Moses, and Israel in prayer? What can we learn from this?

Try This Week

This week as you pray alone, try kneeling or bowing in prayer. After a few days, reflect on how your kneeling or bowing affected your praying.

A Book to Read

Ralph K. Hawkins, *While I Was Praying: Finding Insights about God in Old Testament Prayers* (Macon, GA: Smyth and Helwys, 2006), looks at specific Old Testament prayers in the context of their culture.

CHAPTER 2

"AND HE WILL PRAY FOR YOU"
Prayer as Bold Intercession

"He will pray for you and you will live."

GENESIS 20:7

Augustine was one of the most influential Christians of all times. A monk, a bishop, and a scholar, he cared for the needy, united the church, and left writings that still influence the church today. If you want an example of godly living, you can't do much better than Augustine.

It wasn't always so. Augustine was born into a religiously divided home, his father pagan, his mother Christian. His mother, Monica, taught him the truths of Christ, but they didn't seem to sink in to the young Augustine. For example, he knew that Christ expected chastity of those who were single, but he had a mistress who even bore him a child. Finally, at his mother's urging, he gave up his mistress, but soon had another. According to his autobiography, the *Confessions*, he knew he was sinning and even prayed to God to give him control over his sexual desires. But his prayer was, "Give me chastity and self-control, but not yet," for, as he says, he wanted his lust satisfied, not extinguished.

Augustine wanted to do right, but couldn't. He wanted to resist temptation, but couldn't quite bring himself to give up the pleasures of sin.

What changed Augustine? Many answers could be given: his study of Scripture, his Christian companions, and above all, the power of God. Certainly there was one thing that led to his conversion: in spite of all his sins, his mother Monica never stopped praying for him. After long years, her prayers were answered. Augustine was converted and became the great bishop and theologian that the world respects today.

Who prays for you? What would you be today without the prayers of a mother, a father, a wife, a husband, or a friend? How often have we all received strength from God by the intercession of others? Perhaps we'll never know.

More importantly, for whom do you pray? Have your prayers progressed from selfish requests to intercession for others? When you bow to pray, is your first thought of yourself? Of God? Of others?

We need to learn how to go to God on behalf of those we love, yes, even on behalf of those who hate us. We learn from Jesus, who, even from the cross, prayed for those who put him there: "Father, forgive them, for they do not know what they are doing" (Luke 23:34). We also can learn from the faithful of the Old Testament, who prayed for friends and relatives, but also interceded with God for their enemies.

Significantly, most prayers in the Pentateuch are intercessory prayers. When we open our Bibles, we first see people praying not for themselves, but for others. Certainly it is not wrong to ask God for what you need—Jesus taught us to ask for our daily bread—but one with a mature faith will grab the opportunity to call God's blessings down on others. Here God treats us as his confidant and partner. We cooperate with him to bless others.

What keeps us from praying for others? Perhaps our own selfishness. Our indifference. Our lack of time or lack of discipline. Maybe we fear our prayers will not be answered or (what is more frightening) that God may want us to help those for whom we pray. Praying for others can be dangerous. Or perhaps there are genuine questions we have about this whole enterprise of intercessory prayer. If so, the intercessory prayers of the Pentateuch can help answer those questions.

Does It Do Any Good to Pray for Others?

We may fail to pray for others because we wonder if it really does any good. After all, isn't everyone responsible for himself? Shouldn't people pray for their own troubles? Doesn't God know better than we what other people need? Isn't God a just God who will give folks what they need without us asking for them?

Abraham must have faced these same questions, for he too comes to wrestle with the question of God's justice. God had seen the wickedness of Sodom and decided in his righteous justice to destroy them. He does not hide this decision from Abraham, for Abraham cares about the fate of Sodom since his nephew Lot lives there (see Genesis 13:12). When Abraham is told of God's decision about Sodom, he is bold enough to intercede for the city.

The men turned away and went toward Sodom, but Abraham remained standing before the Lord. Then Abraham approached him and said: "Will you sweep away the righteous with the wicked? What if there are fifty righteous people in the city? Will you really sweep it away and not spare the place for the sake of the fifty righteous people in it? Far be it from you to do such a thing—to kill the righteous with the wicked, treating the righteous and the wicked alike. Far be it from you! Will not the Judge of all the earth do right?"

The Lord said, "If I find fifty righteous people in the city of Sodom, I will spare the whole place for their sake."

Then Abraham spoke up again: "Now that I have been so bold as to speak to the Lord, though I am nothing but dust and ashes, what if the number of the righteous is five less than fifty? Will you destroy the whole city because of five people?" "If I find forty-five there," he said, "I will not destroy it."

Once again he spoke to him, "What if only forty are found there?"

He said, "For the sake of forty, I will not do it."

Then he said, "May the Lord not be angry, but let me speak. What if only thirty can be found there?"

He answered, "I will not do it if I find thirty there."

Abraham said, "Now that I have been so bold as to speak to the Lord, what if only twenty can be found there?"

He said, "For the sake of twenty, I will not destroy it."

Then he said, "May the Lord not be angry, but let me speak just oncemore. What if only ten can be found there?"

He answered, "For the sake of ten, I will not destroy it." (Genesis 18:22-32)

Here is amazing boldness in intercession. Abraham actually bargains with the Lord Almighty! And the Lord bargains back! Abraham puts his very being on the line for Sodom. He even risks making God angry at him in order to plead for the evil city. And God hears! He makes the bargain to spare Sodom for the sake of ten righteous people.

Yet Sodom is still destroyed. Not even ten righteous can be found. So the question comes again, "Does it do any good to intercede for others in prayer?" Did Abraham's bold prayer actually accomplish anything, since Sodom is destroyed?

Yes, at least two things are accomplished through this prayer. One, God does "bargain" with Abraham, that is, he allows Abraham's prayer to affect his will toward Sodom. It's not God's fault (nor Abraham's) that ten righteous are not to be found in the city. If there had been ten, he would have spared the city as he promised. Secondly, God does spare someone from the city; he spares Lot and his family. This is in answer to Abraham's prayer, for "when God destroyed the cities of the plain, he remembered Abraham, and he brought Lot out of the catastrophe that overthrew the cities where Lot had lived" (Genesis 19:29).

God remembered Abraham. This is the lesson we can learn about intercessory prayer: when we pray for others, God hears us, he remembers us, he answers us. We can always be bold in prayer to God, but (like Abraham) we can be particularly bold in praying for others. Intercessory prayer can even change the mind and action of God.

Do you ever fail to pray for others because you think their situation hopeless? I have some close friends who are having marital trouble. Their problems are long-term and deep-seated. Divorce seems inevitable. I try to pray for them, but part of me says it's wasted effort; no power can put this marriage back together. Their fate is fixed.

Then I remember Abraham. God spoke as if his will was fixed: "Sodom will be destroyed." But Abraham is both humble and bold before God. He pleads repeatedly for Sodom. He is heard. If Abraham can turn away God's wrath from Sodom, if his prayer caused Lot to be spared, then surely I can pray for my friends. The One who rescued Lot will rescue them. When destruction of a city or a marriage or of anything seems inevitable, God has the power to save. We come to that power in intercessory prayer.

Doesn't Intercession Make Us Look Hypocritical?

We may fail to pray for others because we're afraid it makes us look spiritually superior to them. Praying for an evil Sodom is easy, for no matter how sinful we are, we're at least better than they. More difficult is to pray for those who are more spiritually mature. Why should we intercede for them? Shouldn't we instead ask them to pray for us?

One of the more obscure Abraham stories teaches us otherwise. Abraham and his wife Sarah had moved to Gerar. Abraham lied about Sarah and said she was his sister, not his wife. We're not told why he did this. Perhaps he was afraid that the king of Gerar, Abimelech, would want Sarah as his wife and would kill Abraham to get her. In fact, Abimelech did want Sarah and brought her into the royal court, intending to marry her. He did this innocently since he believed she was Abraham's sister and unmarried.

Innocent or not, it was wrong to marry a woman who was already married, so God punished Abimelech by making his harem barren. God even threatened Abimelech's life: "You are as good as dead because of the woman you have taken; she is a married woman" (Genesis 20:3). Abimelech proclaims his innocence. God replies:

Then God said to him in the dream, "Yes, I know you did this with a clear conscience, and so I have kept you from sinning against me. This is why I did not let you touch her. Now return the man's wife, for he is a prophet, and he will pray for you and you will live. But if you do not return her, you may be sure that you and yours will die." (Genesis 20:6-7)

Here is a strange twist. Abraham's lie is the cause of all this trouble, yet Abimelech is told by God to ask Abraham to intercede for him. And he does! "Then Abraham prayed to God, and God healed Abimelech, his wife, and his slave girls so they could have children again, for the Lord had closed up every womb in Abimelech's household because of Abraham's wife Sarah" (Genesis 20:17-18).

Surely this is one of the strangest prayer texts in the Bible. Abraham intercedes for another, even though he is in the wrong. What can we possibly learn about prayer from this story? We learn that the power of intercessory prayer is found in our relationship to God, not in the quantity of our righteousness. In this case, Abimelech is more innocent than Abraham, but what Abraham has is a covenant with God. In the same way we can and should pray for those who are more innocent, more righteous, and more spiritual than we. God will hear us, weak though we are, because he has made a covenant with us.

Isn't It Selfish to Intercede for Those Close to Us?

Many of us worry about being selfish in our prayers. One would think those worries have no place in intercessory prayer. After all, aren't we praying for others, not ourselves? Ah, but what about prayers for those closest to us, our wife, husband, children, parents, friends? Can't those prayers be selfish?

Perhaps, but I'm not sure we should worry so much about such selfishness. Even if our prayer for others is also what our hearts desire, we should not fail to pray. Rebekah had one desire deep in her heart: she wanted a child. "Isaac prayed to the Lord on behalf of his wife, because she was barren. The Lord answered his prayer, and his wife Rebekah became pregnant" (Genesis 25:21).

Isaac's prayer is answered even though his desire for a child was probably as strong as Rebekah's. Is this then a selfish prayer? No, for there are times when our heart's desire is the same as God's will for us. Indeed, we are reminded in this passage that the power of life is in God's hands not ours. These children, Jacob and Esau, are not only born, but called. They live because prayers are answered. This is true of all children. They are brought into the world not just as a result of our desires, but as a gift of God.

Thus even when we pray for what we want most, our focus should be on God's power and will, not on our desires. We can intercede for the life and good of wife, husband, child, parent, and friend, knowing that God's desire for their good is even greater than our own.

Can We Sincerely Intercede for Those Who Mean Us Harm?

"Love your enemies," Jesus said, "and pray for those who persecute you" (Matthew 5:43). Much easier said than done. But the idea of praying for your enemies is also found in the Old Testament. God's people had no greater enemy in the Old Testament than Pharaoh. He kept them in slavery and even made their work harder when they complained of their lot. God called Moses to confront Pharaoh and demand that he let Israel go. God put teeth into that command by bringing the Ten Plagues upon the Egyptians.

It is therefore surprising to find Moses praying for Pharaoh and the Egyptians. After the plagues of frogs (Exodus 8:8-15), flies (Exodus 8:28-32), hail (Exodus 9:27-35), and locusts (Exodus 10:10-20), Pharaoh promises to let the people go and begs

Moses to intercede with God to end the plagues. Each time Moses prays, God answers, the plague stops, and Pharaoh changes his mind.

What can we learn about prayer from such a story? It seems far removed from our lives. Yet we all have people who mean us harm, perhaps in government bureaucracies, on the job, or even in our churches and families. How do we treat them? Not by taking personal vengeance but by relying on a just God. Even when God punishes and plagues them, we pray for their repentance. We even intercede with God for them.

But what if they only pretend repentance and turn on us again? We continue to pray for them. Moses and (more importantly) God had patience with Pharaoh. That patience is not unlimited but it is amazingly long. The story of Moses interceding for Pharaoh illustrates the later teaching of Jesus that we should pray for our enemies and forgive them even seventy-seven times (Matthew 18:22). We intercede for our enemies as well as for those closest to us.

Are There Sins That Are Beyond Intercession?

Some sins are so extreme that we may hesitate to intercede for those who commit them. Should we pray for a mass murderer even if he repents? How about a child abuser? A rapist? These are the most heinous crimes in our society. They were some of the most serious ones in Israel. But there was another offense as bad or worse to the Israelites: turning from God to idols.

God leads Israel from Egypt with a mighty hand. He brings them to Sinai to give them his instruction and make them his people. At the heart of God's instruction to his children are the Ten Commandments. While Moses is on the mountain receiving the first two commandments, "You shall have no other Gods before me," and "You shall not make for yourself an idol," the Israelites are in the valley making and worshipping a golden calf (Exodus 32). Can there be a greater sin than this—ingratitude, rebellion, and idolatry? No wonder Moses throws down and breaks the stone tablets of the Law in his anger. No wonder God says to Moses, "Now leave me alone so that my anger may burn against them and that I may destroy them" (Exodus 32:10).

But Moses will not leave God alone. He dares to fall face down before the Lord and intercedes for Israel and for Aaron (Exodus 34:8-9; Deuteronomy 9:18-20). God hears his cry and removes the punishment from Israel. He calls Moses back to the mountain and gives him the Law anew.

This is not the last time Moses will intercede for his people. They soon forget the deliverance from Egypt and the lessons of Sinai. They again show ingratitude toward God by complaining of the hardships of their journey. In his righteous anger, God burns the outskirts of Israel's camp. Moses again intercedes and the fire dies down (Numbers 11:1-3).

How do the Israelites react to the prayerful intercession of Moses? With gratitude? With loyalty? No. At least some rebel against Moses. Korah, Dathan, Abiram, along with 250 Israelite leaders reject the leadership of Moses and Aaron. Again God's anger burns against Israel and he threatens to destroy them all. Again Moses intercedes and God confines his punishment to the leaders of the rebellion (Numbers 16:1-35).

The pattern repeats. Israel again grumbles. God sends poisonous snakes to punish them. They repent and ask Moses to intercede. He prays for them again and God hears. He tells Moses to make a bronze snake and place it on a pole. All those bitten who look at it are cured (Numbers 21:4-9).

Why does Moses keep praying for these rebellious people? More importantly, why does God keep forgiving them? The answer lies in the character of Moses and the character of God. God forgives Israel for the sake of Moses. A righteous person can intercede for the worst of sinners. God also forgives them and us for his own sake. He is a righteous, faithful, and merciful God who is slow to anger and quick to forgive.

Don't Stop Praying for Others

What can we learn about prayer from such old stories? We learn that we should never stop praying for others. Prayer is not just a way to get our way with God. It's the way we let God have his way with us. When he has his way, we begin to think less often of ourselves and care instead for those around us. It is right to intercede for those closest to our hearts. It is right to pray for those who harm us. It is right to pray for the worst of sinners if they want to turn back to God.

In prayer we contact the very will of God. In intercessory prayer we are given the unbelievable privilege of affecting the will of God. We dare not neglect that privilege. Have you prayed for someone lately? God is waiting to hear from you.

Questions for Further Discussion

1. Should we bargain with God in prayer as Abraham did for Sodom? Why or why not? Did Abraham's prayer do any good?

2. Can we intercede for those who are better people than we are? Will God hear such a prayer? Why or why not?

3. Is praying for those closest to us selfish? Will God hear that kind of prayer?

4. Isn't it hypocritical to intercede for our enemies? Can we honestly pray for those who mean us harm?

5. Are there sins people commit that are so horrible that we should not pray for them? Should we pray for those who will not repent?

Try This Week

Write a list of the people you want to pray for each week. Daily, as you pray, run your finger down each name on the list. At the end of the week reflect on how this practice affected your intercession.

A Book to Read

The most helpful scholarly book on Old Testament prayer is Patrick Miller, *They Cried to the Lord: The Form and Theology of Biblical Prayer* (Minneapolis: Fortress Press, 1994).

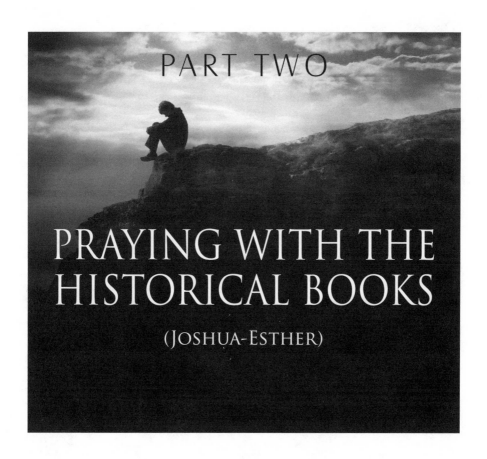

PART TWO

PRAYING WITH THE HISTORICAL BOOKS

(JOSHUA-ESTHER)

Chapter 3

"Oh Lord, I Beg You"
Prayer as Life-Changing Requests to God

*"Go in peace, and may the God of Israel
grant you what you have asked of him."*

1 Samuel 1:17

What is it we really want? What do we desire more than anything in the world?
What hunger occupies most of our waking moments?

Should we ask God to give us what we want?

Praying for others seems so unselfish, so like God himself. Asking for what we
desire seems so self-centered. Should we pour out our desires to God in prayer or
keep them bottled up inside?

The answer, of course, is "It depends." There are prayers that are selfish and harm-
ful. If our desires are out of control, we should not expect God to give us what we
ask. Even as human fathers and mothers, we know it is not best to give our children
everything they ask for. On the other hand, we would think it strange and unhealthy
if our children never asked us for anything.

It's the same way between God and us. He is a Father, not a dispenser of good-
ies. Yet, as a Father, he wants to know our desires. He wants to give us what we want,
if it is best for us. In the Old Testament, God's children boldly made their requests

to God, pouring out the deepest desires of their hearts. God the loving Father heard them, and granted their requests.

For a Child

Many of us know what it's like to want a child. We hunger to have a little boy or girl to love and to nurture. In the world of ancient Israel, the thinking of the culture enhanced that natural desire. Children were a blessing of God. They were the only sure way to immortality promised in the Old Testament, a way to carry on the family name. In that culture, people literally lived through their children.

Most considered the inability to have children a curse from God, particularly for women. The pain of social pressure compounded the frustration of being childless. That pain and frustration is exactly what Hannah felt. She had a good marriage (at least good for the days of polygamy). She was her husband's favorite wife. But her rival, his other wife Peninnah, had given her husband Elkanah children. Hannah could not.

Elkanah said the right things. "Don't cry, Hannah. Don't I mean more to you than ten sons?" But he could not console her. In her pain, she goes to the tabernacle of the Lord at Shiloh and pours out her request to God.

> In bitterness of soul Hannah wept much and prayed to the Lord. And she
> made a vow, saying, "O Lord Almighty, if you will only look upon your ser-
> vant's misery and remember me, and not forget your servant but give her a
> son, then I will give him to the Lord for all the days of his life, and no razor
> will ever be used on his head." (1 Samuel 1:10-11)

Hannah not only prays for what she wants, she also makes a bargain with God: "If you give me this child, I will give him back to your service."

Is this an example for us? Are we to bargain with God? Won't God give us what we want and need without our making deals with him?

Certainly he will. I don't think Hannah's prayer teaches us that we have to bargain with God. It might teach us something about selfish and unselfish prayer. Hannah wants a son more than anything in the world. Yet, she is willing to give that son in service to God. She doesn't want him merely for herself. She wants him for God's sake.

When we ask for our deepest desires, one desire must be deepest of all—the desire to do God's will. We must use whatever God gives us—health, life, houses, children—in his service and to his glory. Hannah knew this secret of prayer.

Hannah's prayer is also interesting because she gets in trouble for praying! She prays silently, what must have been an unusual way for her time. As a result, Eli the priest thinks she is in a drunken stupor, not a spiritual struggle.

> As she kept on praying to the Lord, Eli observed her mouth. Hannah was praying in her heart, and her lips were moving but her voice was not heard. Eli thought she was drunk and said to her, "How long will you keep on getting drunk? Get rid of your wine."
>
> "Not so, my lord," Hannah replied, "I am a woman who is deeply troubled. I have not been drinking wine or beer; I was pouring out my soul to the Lord. Do not take your servant for a wicked woman; I have been praying here out of my great anguish and grief."
>
> Eli answered, "Go in peace, and may the God of Israel grant you what you have asked of him." (1 Samuel 1:12-17)

To his credit, Eli quickly realizes his mistake and blesses Hannah. Has anyone ever misconstrued your prayers? Perhaps at times we use an unusual posture or language that confuses others. There's nothing wrong with that if we, like Hannah, can correct that misconception, but at times we cannot. Prayer can be perilous to our reputations with certain people. There is also a warning here against too quickly judging the praying of others just because it is different from the norm.

The greatest lesson to learn from Hannah is that she prayed in faith, confident that God would grant her request. She fasted, cried, and prayed, but when her prayer was over, "Then she went her way and ate something, and her face was no longer downcast" (1 Samuel 1:18). Hannah no longer had a reason to grieve for she knew God had heard her request. Hers is a great example of the peace that comes through trusting prayer. She and Elkanah have a son named Samuel. He would be one of the greatest leaders God's people had ever known—all because of the prayer of a faithful woman and the gift of a gracious God.

For Guidance

Hannah isn't the only woman to feel the sting of being childless. Earlier a man named Manoah and his wife can have no children. The angel of the Lord appears to the wife, announcing they will have a son. When his wife tells Manoah, he immediately prays for guidance. "Then Manoah prayed to the Lord: 'O Lord, I beg you, let the man of God you sent us come again to teach us how to bring up the boy who is to be born" (Judges 13:8).

God grants Manoah's request. The angel appears again and repeats his instruction that their son is to be a Nazirite. He is not to drink wine or cut his hair.

Who was this boy? Samson, the strong hero of Israel. He maintained his strength until he let his hair be cut. If you remember how headstrong (to make a bad pun) Samson was, then no wonder his father felt the need for guidance in raising him.

You may not have given birth to a Samson, but you may have a strong-willed child. It's tough enough giving birth, but don't all parents need guidance in raising their children? How in the world can we keep them safe in a world of evil? How can we raise them in the path of the Lord when our culture has so many snares set for them? Only by the power of God through prayer can we bring up our children in God's way. We need his guidance.

For Healing

One of the more unusual request prayers in the Old Testament is a prayer for healing. What makes it unusual is that the physical ailment comes as a curse from God.

A prophet comes to the unrighteous king Jeroboam and curses the altar Jeroboam had built to pagan gods. When Jeroboam hears the curse, he points to the prophet and says, "Seize him." At that moment the arm he stretched out towards the prophet shrivels up and the altar is split in two.

Having cursed God's prophet and earned a just punishment, Jeroboam then asks the man of God to pray for his arm to be restored. The man prays, God hears, and Jeroboam's hand is as good as new (see 1 Kings 13:1-6).

We could look at this story in a later chapter on repentance and intercession. But it is significant here that God sometimes heals those who bring their problems on themselves. Some may see addictions as just punishment for those without self-control. But God is so gracious that he even heals those who turn against him, provided they turn back.

For Life

What could we want more than children? What can we pray for that is more basic than raising them right? What is even more important than the use of a hand?

How about our own lives? Is it right to pray that God will spare our lives, both for our sake and for others?

Hezekiah thought so. He was so bold in prayer that he even asked God to change his mind.

> In those days Hezekiah became ill and was at the point of death. The prophet
> Isaiah son of Amoz went to him and said, "This is what the Lord says: Put
> your house in order, because you are going to die; you will not recover."
>
> Hezekiah turned his face to the wall and prayed to the Lord, "Remember,
> O Lord, how I have walked before you faithfully and with wholehearted
> devotion and have done what is good in your eyes." And Hezekiah wept
> bitterly. (2 Kings 20:1-3)

Perhaps, like Hezekiah, you've faced impending death from disease or accident. All of us have had loved ones whom doctors have pronounced terminal. How do we pray when death seems so certain?

It is not a physician but the Almighty himself through the prophet Isaiah who pronounces Hezekiah's death sentence. If God himself says we are going to die, shouldn't we accept it?

Perhaps. But Hezekiah audaciously pours out his heart to God with tears. He doesn't want to die! He reminds God of his faithful service. And God hears! The Almighty changes his mind and spares Hezekiah's life.

> Before Isaiah had left the middle court, the word of the Lord came to him:
> "Go back and tell Hezekiah, the leader of my people, 'This is what the Lord,
> the God of your father David, says: I have heard your prayer and seen your
> tears; I will heal you. On the third day from now you will go up to the temple
> of the Lord. I will add fifteen years to your life. And I will deliver you and
> this city from the hand of the king of Assyria. I will defend this city for my
> sake and for the sake of my servant David.'" (2 Kings 20:4-6)

God grants Hezekiah's heart-felt request and gives him fifteen more years. Why? Not only because of Hezekiah's faithfulness, but because of God's promise to David and to Israel.

What can we learn about prayer from this example? When our loved ones are terminally ill, will God always grant them life? We know better. Should we then give up on them, or rather, give up on God? Never. For God has life in his hands. He may hear our prayers and tears and give us more years of service.

I just received a message from Stan, a former student and current friend. A few months ago, Stan's dad received his own announcement of death, a diagnosis of advanced pancreatic cancer. How did Stan and his family and friends react? With prayer. We prayed for the life of Stan's father. Yesterday's message from Stan said his father's treatment and surgery was completely successful. The cancer is gone!

How do we explain that? Good doctors? Yes. Wise treatment? Of course. But I think God spared the life of Stan's father, giving him months and years of future service.

But this prayer of Hezekiah also reminds of a time when God did not spare the life of one who prayed to him "with loud cries and tears" (Hebrews 5:7). In the garden, Jesus prayed the prayer of Hezekiah. But what Jesus wanted even more than life was for God's will to be done. We should always be bold to ask for life. Who knows, like Hezekiah, we might even change the will of God. But we must also always pray knowing that God's will is always for our ultimate good. We pray knowing that our Father knows best. Yet in prayer, as children of God, we should never hide the deepest desires of our hearts. God may give life.

For Resurrection

Two of the prayer requests in this chapter, for children and for life, come together in another biblical story. This time an unnamed woman from Shunem is childless and both she and her husband are old. However, this woman shows hospitality to Elisha the prophet, so he wants to show his gratitude. He promises the couple a son. Sure enough, a year later, they have a little boy.

All is well until one day the boy runs out to meet his father in the field, crying, "My head! My head!" A servant takes the boy to his mother. He sits on her lap until noon, then dies in her arms.

What can be worse than the death of a child? Any child. Particularly an unexpected child, born after his parents had given up all hope of having children. Would it not have been better for Elisha (and God) to have left these poor people alone than to raise then dash their hopes?

But this is not the end of the story. This heartbroken, bitter woman rides off to find the prophet. When she meets Elisha, she asks, "Did I ask you for a son, my lord?

Didn't I tell you, 'Don't raise my hopes'?" (2 Kings 4:28). Is there a sadder cry in all the Bible?

Elisha sends his servant Gehazi to lay his staff on the dead boy. He does. Nothing happens. Dead is dead. Hope is lost.

But no.

> When Elisha reached the house, there was the boy lying dead on his couch. He went in, shut the door on the two of them and prayed to the Lord. Then he got on the bed and lay upon the boy, mouth to mouth, eyes to eyes, hands to hands. As he stretched himself out upon him, the boy's body grew warm. Elisha turned away and walked back and forth in the room and then got on the bed and stretched out upon him once more. The boy sneezed seven times and opened his eyes.
>
> Elisha summoned Gehazi and said, "Call the Shunammite." And he did. When she came, he said, "Take your son." She came in, fell at his feet and bowed to the ground. Then she took her son and went out. (2 Kings 4:32-37)

From tragedy comes triumph. From death, resurrection.

All through prayer.

Is this kind of prayer for us? I know two families whose daughters received a cancer diagnosis at the same time. Both are Christian families. In each case hundreds of prayers went up to the father for a cure. One girl survived. The other didn't. What should the parents and friends of the dead girl pray for? Resurrection?

Exactly. We do not expect our loved ones to rise off their deathbeds like this little boy. We do expect, because we have the promise, that they will live again at the last day.

So what does this story teach us about prayer now? We pray to the God of all power. The God who raised this boy will raise our children and mothers and fathers, yes and even us. There is nothing, not even death, that is beyond the power of the gracious God. He is a God who gives and a God who keeps his promises. We claim those promises in prayer.

Pray for What You Want

From these stories we learn that it is not wrong to pray for what we want most— children, healing, and life. We should not hide our deepest desires from God, thinking they are not worthy. God wants to give us the desires of our hearts. More than that, he wants to shape us until we want one thing most of all—to do his will. We pray with boldness, confident that our loving Father always listens and always wants to give us what we need most.

Questions for Further Discussion

1. Is it wrong to pray for what we want? Could it be wrong? Is it more spiritual to pray for others rather than for yourself?

2. What happens when we pray for children and still cannot have any? Is this a curse from God?

3. Specifically, what kinds of guidance do we need in raising children? What do you pray for regarding your kids?

4. Is it right to pray for God to spare our lives? What happens if God spares us and then we turn against him? Are some things worse than death?

5. Should we pray for resurrection? Isn't that a sure promise from God through Christ?

Try This Week

Ask yourself what you worry about the most. This week, pray about that daily. When you pray, release your worries to God. At the end of the week, see if your anxiety has diminished.

A Book to Read

Another book that looks at prayer in both Old and New Testaments is Wilfrid Harrington, *The Bible's Ways of Prayer* (Wilmington, Del.: Michael Glazier, 1980). It is out of print but one can find a copy online and in used book stores.

Chapter 4

"Do Not Stop Crying Out to the Lord"

Prayer as a Cry for Deliverance

"Do not stop crying out to the Lord our God for us, that he may rescue us."

1 Samuel 7:8

Who are your enemies?

"I don't have any!" you reply. "After all, aren't Christians supposed to love everyone? Should we have enemies?"

Didn't Jesus love everyone? Didn't he have enemies who hated him so much that they put him on a cross? Are we better than Jesus?

No. The student is not greater than the teacher. If Jesus had enemies, then Christians will, too.

So who are our enemies? Perhaps those at work who make fun of us behind our backs, or sometimes to our faces, because of our strange practices. Practices like abstaining from premarital or extra-marital sex, drunkenness, and foul language. Practices like prayer, Bible study, and regular church attendance. Some hate us because we show kindness to others, particularly those different from us.

Does someone hate you for being a Christian? Don't we have enemies? If so, how should we treat them? Jesus says to love them. Not *like* them, that's impossible, but to desire their good. Jesus said to pray for our enemies. It is also right to pray for deliverance from our enemies. Perhaps you remember the prayer for the Tsar in the play "Fiddler on the Roof," "May God keep the Tsar . . . far from us." That's the kind of prayer we find often in the Old Testament.

The God of Battle

It is difficult to translate the experience of Israel into our own time. As God's chosen people, Israel faced national enemies. This was more than political clashes or human warfare. It was a contest of gods. Who was more powerful, the gods of the nations or the Lord God of Israel?

The Philistines were one of the perpetual enemies of Israel. At the height of their power, their army seemed overwhelming and unbeatable. They faced Israel at Mizpah, and Israel reacted with fear.

> When the Philistines heard that Israel had assembled at Mizpah, the rulers of the Philistines came up to attack them. And when the Israelites heard of it, they were afraid because of the Philistines. They said to Samuel, "Do not stop crying out to the Lord our God for us, that he may rescue us from the hand of the Philistines." Then Samuel took a suckling lamb and offered it up as a whole burnt offering to the Lord. He cried out to the Lord on Israel's behalf, and the Lord answered him. (1 Samuel 7:7-9)

There were times when Israel trusted in her own strength, in the number of soldiers and weapons she possessed. Here Israel faces overwhelming odds. The nation cries out to Samuel to intercede for them with God, asking for deliverance from her enemies. God answers in dramatic fashion.

> While Samuel was sacrificing the burnt offering, the Philistines drew near to engage Israel in battle. But that day the Lord thundered with loud thunder against the Philistines and threw them into such a panic that the Israelites routed them. The men of Israel rushed out of Mizpah and pursued the Philistines, slaughtering them along the way to a point below Beth Car. (1 Samuel 7:10-11)

Dare we ask God to thunder against our enemies? I think the answer is "Yes," that is, if we understand who our true enemies are. We should not apply these passages about Israel's enemies to our nation's enemies. God has not chosen America or any other nation. The holy nation, chosen of God, in the New Testament consists of those of every nation, tribe, and tongue whose citizenship is in heaven. In light of Jesus' teaching to love our enemies, should we pray for God to thunder against them? Only if we also pray that God will turn their hearts and bless.

So how can we pray the prayer for thundering deliverance? Only by remembering our true enemies. "For our struggle is not against flesh and blood, but against the rulers, against the authorities, against the powers of this dark world and against the spiritual forces of evil in the heavenly realms" (Ephesians 6:12). Evil forces stand against us, overwhelming forces we cannot defeat. But God can. He will, if we, like Israel rely on his power through prayer.

After God defeats the Philistines, Samuel builds a stone memorial of the occasion, calling it "Ebenezer," the stone of help. He adds, "Thus far has the Lord helped us" (1 Samuel 7:12). When God does deliver us from evil, do we take it for granted? Or like Samuel, do we remember the Lord for his help and react with praise and service?

Opening Our Eyes

It seems glib and easy to say that God is our helper. It becomes more difficult when we focus on the evil powers that surround us. Just read the papers. There is war and famine. Children are abused. Murderers go free. Honest business people face ruin because they will not operate unethically like many businesses.

We sometimes face those evil forces personally. What are the names of those principalities and powers we face? They sometimes show themselves as temptations, addictions, and depression. They attack us at our weakest points—our sexuality, our appetites, our self-image. In the hour of trial, as we face a spiritual battle, the odds seem so stacked against us. How can we face such powerful foes?

We need a special sight. We need to focus not on the power of the enemy but on the forces on our side. Elisha's servant needed that vision. One morning he awoke to find himself surrounded by Aramean warriors, horses, and chariots.

When the servant of the man of God got up and went out early the next morning, an army with horses and chariots had surrounded the city. "Oh, my lord, what shall we do?" the servant asked.

"Don't be afraid," the prophet answered. "Those who are with us are more than those who are with them."

And Elisha prayed, "O Lord, open his eyes so he may see." Then the Lord opened the servant's eyes, and he looked and saw the hills full of horses and chariots of fire all around Elisha. (2 Kings 6:15-17)

When surrounded by foes within and without, we may live in fear. This passage reminds us that we have more for us than against us. "You, dear children, are from God and have overcome them, because the one in you is greater than the one who is in the world" (1 John 4:4). In the time of our deepest struggles, God surrounds us with heavenly warriors, horses, and chariots of fire. What we need is to pray God will open our eyes.

After his servant sees the fiery chariots, Elisha prays again, this time that God will blind the Aramean soldiers. God hears, answers, and saves Elisha, his servant, and Israel.

In a similar story, Sennacherib the king of Assyria sends a letter to King Hezekiah, warning that the God of Israel cannot save them from the might of the Assyrian army. Hezekiah prays. He admits that the Assyrians are mighty, but asks, "Now, O Lord our God, deliver us from his hand, so all kingdoms on earth may know that you alone, O Lord, are God" (2 Kings 19:19). God sends Isaiah the prophet to tell Hezekiah that he has been heard and that God will deliver Israel.

Who sees the real world? Those who oppose Christianity? They claim that we Christians blind ourselves to reality. "Why believe in a God you can't see? Wake up and face the facts. Why deny yourself pleasures you can see and feel for the sake of a heaven that's not real?" They may even ridicule our God as powerless in the face of overwhelming evil.

But they are the blind ones. By faith and the power of God through prayer, we can see a spiritual realm, an eternal kingdom, and a fiery army those around us cannot see. We should never contrast "spiritual" with "real." We Christians live in the real world, the world that includes the spiritual armies of the Lord, there to fight for us. The Lord will destroy all the powers that threaten our life in him.

Personal Enemies

But what about our personal enemies? What about those people who just don't like us? The neighborhood kid who ruins our mailboxes for the fun of it. The woman at work who plots behind our backs. The guy who cheats us on our insurance and laughs all the way to the bank. What do we pray concerning those, perhaps even in our own families, who intentionally mean us harm?

David knew what that was like. His own son, Absalom, rebelled against him, claiming the throne for himself. Instead of showing loyalty in such a crisis, one of David's trusted advisors, Ahithophel, threw his support behind Absalom.

What should David do? Whine? Feel sorry for himself? He does cry, not because he feels sorry for himself, but as a sign of humility and repentance toward God. Should David take personal vengeance? No. He puts this situation in the hands of God. When betrayed by those closest to him, David prays.

> But David continued up the Mount of Olives, weeping as he went; his head was covered and he was barefoot. All the people with him covered their heads too and were weeping as they went up. Now David had been told, "Ahithophel is among the conspirators with Absalom." So David prayed, "O Lord, turn Ahithophel's counsel into foolishness." (2 Samuel 15:30-31)

Note that David does not pray for personal revenge, but that Ahithophel's advice will not cause harm to David or his people. This is a version of praying that our enemies will not triumph over us. That kind of prayer about our enemies is always right.

God hears David's prayer, but answers it in an unexpected way. Ahithophel actually gives good advice to Absalom. If Absalom had followed his advice, he would have triumphed over David. But God works it so that Absalom listens instead to the poor advice of Hushai. As a result, Absalom loses and David keeps his throne.

How do we pray for our enemies, for those who harm us for no reason? We pray that God will forgive them. We pray he will turn their hearts toward him. We pray good, not evil for them. But we also pray that God will protect us from their evil schemes.

But can we really pray for those who do us a world of hurt? We can, by the power of God. Joe and Geneva Huber know what it's like to have enemies. A few years ago, they received the call all parents dread. Their middle-aged son, Larry, had been shot and killed on the streets of Nashville by three teenage boys. As Christians, Joe and Geneva prayed for those boys who murdered their son. But they did more than pray for them in word; they also appeared in court pleading for leniency for them. God's love can fill our hearts as it did with Joe and Geneva, fill it so much that we can do good to those who have done us harm.

David knew that love of God. He did not pray for Ahithophel's destruction, but that his advice would not harm others. The Hubers know the love of God. May we know it, even for our enemies.

Protect Ourselves?

Dare we rely on God alone to protect us from those who mean us harm or do we protect ourselves? Is it a sign of distrust of God to have bolt locks and alarm systems on our doors? Is it foolish not to take those precautions?

When a small group of Jews returned from exile to rebuild the walls of Jerusalem, powerful enemies surrounded them. What did they do to protect themselves from those who meant to harm them? They prayed.

But when Sanballat, Tobiah, the Arabs, the Ammonites and the men of Ashdod heard that the repairs to Jerusalem's walls had gone ahead and that the gaps were being closed, they were very angry. They all plotted together to come and fight against Jerusalem and stir up trouble against it. But we prayed to our God and posted a guard day and night to meet this threat. (Nehemiah 4:7-9)

What do we do about those who would harm us? What did Nehemiah and the Jews do? "We prayed to our God and posted a guard." It is not wrong to take precautions against our enemies. Posting guards was the ancient equivalent of locks, alarms, and a security force. We should protect ourselves and our loved ones from harm. However, like these people of God, we must also realize that locks, alarms, and police are not our ultimate protection. God is the one who protects from evil. We ask for that protection in prayer.

Later Ezra leads another group of exiles back to Jerusalem. Along the way, they face a perilous journey. Ezra intentionally does not ask for human guards to protect them. He relies on the one who gives traveling mercies and protects from harm.

There, by the Ahava Canal, I proclaimed a fast, so that we might humble ourselves before our God and ask him for a safe journey for us and our children, with all our possessions. I was ashamed to ask the king for soldiers and horsemen to protect us from enemies on the road, because we had told the king, "The gracious hand of our God is on everyone who looks to him, but his great anger is against all who forsake him." So we fasted and petitioned our God about this, and he answered our prayer. (Ezra 8:21-23)

In Nehemiah, God's people pray and post a guard. In Ezra, they intentionally refuse a guard and rely on prayer alone. Which practice should we follow?

It depends on the circumstances. Nehemiah shows us it is not wrong to take precautions against evil. We can lock our doors, call the police, and take people to court to protect our loved ones from harm. But we do it all with prayer. In other words, we do not rely on human defenders and common sense precautions to keep us safe. Through prayer, we rely on the God of hosts who guards his people.

That means there may be times when we refuse government help and human safety devices. We refuse them as a witness to the world, to show them where our true strength and protection lies.

Deliver Us from Evil

Again, all this talk of danger and enemies may sound like paranoia to us. But both Old and New Testaments speak of a spiritual enemy we all face. "Your enemy the devil prowls around like a roaring lion looking for someone to devour" (1 Peter 5:8). Behind those who would harm us for doing good is our ultimate enemy, the devil himself. How can we defeat him? Only through prayer. That's why Jesus taught his disciples, including us, to pray: "Deliver us from the evil one" (Matthew 6:13). Like Israel of old, we must learn to rely on the power of God to deliver us from every enemy.

Questions for Further Discussion _____

1. Should Christians have enemies? Aren't we supposed to love others as our-selves? What would make someone our enemy?

2. What do we pray concerning our enemies? Can we, like Samuel, pray for God to defeat our enemies when Jesus taught us to love and pray for them?

3. In what sense are our enemies blind to reality? What is it we see that they do not?

4. Is it a sign of distrust of God to have bolt locks and alarm systems on our doors? Is it foolish not to take those precautions? Are there times we should not take such precautions? Why not?

5. Who is our ultimate enemy? How does prayer help defeat him?

Try This Week

Think of someone who has wronged you, perhaps someone you thought you had already forgiven. This week pray daily for that person's well-being. At the end of the week, see if your feelings toward that person have changed.

A Book to Read

A small but helpful out-of-print book is Moshe Greenberg, *Biblical Prose Prayer as a Window to the Popular Religion of Ancient Israel* (Berkeley: University of California Press, 1983). These three lectures provide enlightening insights into the spontaneous spoken prayers of the Old Testament.

CHAPTER 5

"There Is No God Like You"
Prayer as Gratitude and Praise

*"How great you are, O Sovereign Lord! There is no one like you,
and there is no God but you, as we have heard with our own ears."*

2 Samuel 7:22

We cannot figure out God. We cannot fathom his ways. And yet we try. We want to know why things happen. We want to know why our prayers were not answered, at least not how or when we wanted them answered.

But prayer is all about trust. One of the hardest things God's followers must learn is to accept all that happens to us in gratitude and praise. Sometimes that is extremely difficult. Sometimes it is easy. This chapter looks at three instances where God answered prayer with a marvelous gift. When that happens, God's people readily respond with heart-felt praise.

For the Gift of a Child

In an earlier chapter we looked at Hannah's request for a child. Many know the deep hurt of wanting a child and not being able to have one. Hannah knew that hurt.

She not only had to live with disappointment, she had to face taunting from her rival wife who had children.

Why wasn't Hannah blessed with children? Was her faith not strong enough? Was she distant from God? Was God distant from her?

No. She trusted God. And so she prayed earnestly for a child.

But even in her praying, she was misunderstood. She faced undeserved correction. Eli the priest thought she was drunk in the house of God, instead of praying. "Not so, my lord," Hannah replied, "I am a woman who is deeply troubled. I have not been drinking wine or beer; I was pouring out my soul to the Lord. Do not take your servant for a wicked woman; I have been praying here out of my great anguish and grief" (1 Samuel 1:15-16). When he realized his mistake, Eli prayed for Hannah, that the Lord might grant her request.

God heard. God granted. God gave her a son. She named him Samuel, which means, "Heard by God."

But what about those of us who do not get the child we so much want? I know what it is like to lose an unborn child. I know what it is like to be without children. Does God not care? Does God not hear? Is it my own lack of goodness or faith?

These are questions we cannot help but ask. I do not have easy answers to these heart-felt questions. But I am helped by Hannah's reaction to the great gift she has received. She knows that there is a bigger picture. This is not simply about her personal desire for a child. This is about a God who is faithful. So while in an earlier chapter we focused on Hannah's request and God's answer, here the spotlight is on Hannah's reaction to the gift.

Then Hannah prayed and said:

"My heart rejoices in the Lord;
　　in the Lord my horn is lifted high.
My mouth boasts over my enemies,
　　for I delight in your deliverance.
"There is no one holy like the Lord;
　　there is no one besides you;
　　there is no Rock like our God."

(1 Samuel 2:1-2)

If this were Hannah's whole prayer, then it would be a cry of joy to the God who has heard her. However, she has more to say. What God has done is *for* her, but not primarily *about* her. God's action shows what kind of God he is. He is a God who makes things right in his own time. A God of justice. The God of the underdog, the downtrodden, and the poor. A God who is in control, even though it might not always seem that way.

> "Do not keep talking so proudly
>> or let your mouth speak such arrogance,
> for the Lord is a God who knows,
>> and by him deeds are weighed.
> "The bows of the warriors are broken,
>> but those who stumbled are armed with strength.
> Those who were full hire themselves out for food,
>> but those who were hungry hunger no more.
> She who was barren has borne seven children,
>> but she who has had many sons pines away.
> "The Lord brings death and makes alive;
>> he brings down to the grave and raises up.
> The Lord sends poverty and wealth;
>> he humbles and he exalts.
> He raises the poor from the dust
>> and lifts the needy from the ash heap;
> he seats them with princes
>> and has them inherit a throne of honor.
> "For the foundations of the earth are the Lord's;
>> upon them he has set the world.
> He will guard the feet of his saints,
>> but the wicked will be silenced in darkness.
> "It is not by strength that one prevails;
>> those who oppose the Lord will be shattered.
> He will thunder against them from heaven;
>> the Lord will judge the ends of the earth.

"He will give strength to his king
and exalt the horn of his anointed."

(1 SAMUEL 2:3-10)

Hannah gets what she so much wants from God. Some of us have prayed similar prayers and not gotten what we wanted. Still, in faith we can praise the Lord. Like Hannah, we trust that he is the great reverser, the one who exalts the humble and humbles the exalted. We do not see, but we believe that he will make things right.

Why do we believe when we do not see? Why risk trusting a God who does not always give us what we want with all our hearts? The greatest answer is in the last line of Hannah's prayer: "He will give strength to his king and exalt the horn of his anointed." These are strange words for Hannah. She lives before Israel has a king. No doubt these words reflect a later time when Israel prayed for God's anointed king. But they also display the unusual way God works. God begins the story of Israel's king not with pomp and glory but with a powerless woman who pours out her heart to God. From that barren woman God brings forth the future of his people. God gives her a son who will anoint the first two kings of Israel.

Christians cannot hear these words without thinking of the ultimate anointed one, the Christ. Through Jesus, we see God beginning to make the world right. That's why it is significant that there is another prayer like Hannah's in the Bible. When Mary is blessed with the news of a Son, she breaks out in song, the Magnificat, praising God in words much like Hannah's (see Luke 1:46-55).

God does not always give us what we so much want. But he gave himself, God made flesh. The greatest gift of all. The gift that raises the lowly.

For the Gift of a Kingdom

Even though it was not God's original plan for Israel to have kings, he uses those kings for his purposes. The last line of Hannah's prayer reminds us that the king was God's anointed representative. The king was to turn the people's hearts to the Lord.

No king fit that purpose better than David. David did not set out to be king. He was just a shepherd. But when God makes him king, David responds with humility and praise.

Then King David went in and sat before the Lord, and he said: "Who am I, O Sovereign Lord, and what is my family, that you have brought me this far? And as if this were not enough in your sight, O Sovereign Lord, you have also spoken about the future of the house of your servant. Is this your usual way of dealing with man, O Sovereign Lord?

"What more can David say to you? For you know your servant, O Sovereign Lord. For the sake of your word and according to your will, you have done this great thing and made it known to your servant.

"How great you are, O Sovereign Lord! There is no one like you, and there is no God but you, as we have heard with our own ears. And who is like your people Israel—the one nation on earth that God went out to redeem as a people for himself, and to make a name for himself, and to perform great and awesome wonders by driving out nations and their gods from before your people, whom you redeemed from Egypt? You have established your people Israel as your very own forever, and you, O Lord, have become their God. (2 Samuel 7:18-24)

David knows that he is king only by the grace of God. He does not deserve it. He also knows that his success or failure as king is not important. The story of Israel is not about David. It is all about a gracious God.

Some of us may have ambitions to be kings or queens. Our egos are not so big that we think we will rule nations, but we want to rule our own kingdoms—family, business, and church. We think we are in control of our lives.

David knows better. From his prayer we learn that our lives are about God, not primarily about us. We accept whatever roles we have as God's gift. We do not seek to rule, but to praise.

For the Gift of a Temple

Praise to God is a response to the presence of God. Hannah sees God in the gift of a child, so she praises him. David experiences the presence of God in the gift of a kingdom. He gives God the glory. Solomon builds a temple for God. The glory of the Lord fills that temple and Solomon breaks out in praise.

Then Solomon stood before the altar of the Lord in front of the whole assembly of Israel, spread out his hands toward heaven and said:

"O Lord, God of Israel, there is no God like you in heaven above or on earth below—you who keep your covenant of love with your servants who continue wholeheartedly in your way. You have kept your promise to your servant David my father; with your mouth you have promised and with your hand you have fulfilled it—as it is today.

"Now Lord, God of Israel, keep for your servant David my father the promises you made to him when you said, 'You shall never fail to have a man to sit before me on the throne of Israel, if only your sons are careful in all they do to walk before me as you have done.' And now, O God of Israel, let your word that you promised your servant David my father come true.

"But will God really dwell on earth? The heavens, even the highest heaven, cannot contain you. How much less this temple I have built! Yet give attention to your servant's prayer and his plea for mercy, O Lord my God. Hear the cry and the prayer that your servant is praying in your presence this day. May your eyes be open toward this temple night and day, this place of which you said, 'My Name shall be there,' so that you will hear the prayer your servant prays toward this place. Hear the supplication of your servant and of your people Israel when they pray toward this place. Hear from heaven, your dwelling place, and when you hear, forgive." (1 Kings 8:22-30)

Solomon builds a temple for the Lord. Yet he knows that no temple can contain God. Not even the heaven's can contain him! No temple, cathedral, or church—no matter how majestic—can box in God. The temple of Solomon is not intended to contain or control God. It is intended as a place where God's people can be aware of his presence.

God's presence is always around us. We cannot create it. He is there whether we know it or not. Always in, with, under, above, and beside us. But we humans get distracted. We let less important things rob us of our awareness of God. God gives us sacred places to remind us of his presence. Some call these "thin places," where the line between heaven and earth, sacred and secular fades.

The temple was one of those places. The house of God. A God who lives everywhere, but here in a special way. Solomon prays that when the people seek God in the temple, that God will hear. He will forgive, heal, bless, feed, and restore. He will do this not only for Israel, but for all who seek him at the temple (see 1 Kings 8:31-53).

The New Testament teaches us that the ultimate sacred space or thin place is the human heart. God has become flesh in Christ. Jesus has come to live in his followers through the Spirit. As a result, we both individually and collectively are the place where God dwells. "Do you not know that your body is a temple of the Holy Spirit, who is in you, whom you have received from God?" (1 Corinthians 6:19). "Don't you know that you yourselves are God's temple and that God's Spirit lives in you?" (1 Corinthians 3:16).

We are the temple of God. We can approach him with boldness, knowing that he hears and he gives.

So like Solomon, we dedicate a temple. Not a place of stone but one of flesh. We dedicate our hearts and our bodies together to the Lord. And that dedication results in praise.

> When Solomon had finished all these prayers and supplications to the Lord, he rose from before the altar of the Lord, where he had been kneeling with his hands spread out toward heaven. He stood and blessed the whole assembly of Israel in a loud voice, saying:
>
> "Praise be to the Lord, who has given rest to his people Israel just as he promised. Not one word has failed of all the good promises he gave through his servant Moses. May the Lord our God be with us as he was with our fathers; may he never leave us nor forsake us. May he turn our hearts to him, to walk in all his ways and to keep the commands, decrees and regulations he gave our fathers. And may these words of mine, which I have prayed before the Lord, be near to the Lord our God day and night, that he may uphold the cause of his servant and the cause of his people Israel according to each day's need, so that all the peoples of the earth may know that the Lord is God and that there is no other. But your hearts must be fully committed to the Lord our God, to live by his decrees and obey his commands, as at this time." (1 Kings 8:54-61)

We are God's temple. But as talk of an anointed king reminds us of Jesus the Messiah (or anointed one), so talk of a temple reminds us that Jesus is the ultimate temple of God. God completely lives in him. That's why Jesus can speak of his body as God's temple (John 2:20-22). When Hannah gives thanks for a king, David gives thanks for a kingdom, and Solomon gives thanks for a temple, their gratitude pales beside our thanks for Jesus, our king and our temple. We show that gratitude through prayerful obedience.

Questions for Further Discussion

1. Was Hannah's prayer for a child a selfish prayer? Is it wrong to pray for what we want so much?

2. Can we genuinely praise God when we are disappointed that he has not given us what we ask for? How can that be honest praise?

3. Did David deserve to be king? Do we deserve our blessings? If not, how does that affect our praise?

4. Where do you find it easy to be aware of God? What is a sacred place for you? What makes it that way?

5. What does it mean for us to be the temple of God? How do we live as his temple?

Try This Week

Think of a place nearby where you usually are particularly aware of God's presence. Go there and pray this week. Afterward, ask yourself why you particularly find it easy to praise God in that place.

A Book to Read

For a more topical look at Old Testament prayers, see Michael E.W. Thompson, *I Have Heard Your Prayer: The Old Testament and Prayer* (Peterborough, Eng.: Epworth Press, 1996).

Chapter 6

"LET US FALL INTO THE HANDS OF THE LORD"
Prayers of Heartfelt Repentance

"I have sinned greatly in what I have done. Now, O Lord, I beg you, take away the guilt of your servant. I have done a very foolish thing."

2 SAMUEL 24:10

Prayer is turning our hearts toward God. Sometimes, it is turning our hearts and our lives back to God. The Historical Books of the Old Testament give many examples of those who turned against the will of God, suffered punishment, then turned back to God. Like them, we too need to admit our sins, ask for grace, and embrace the forgiveness of a loving God. No matter how embarrassing the sin, God will forgive, accept, and embrace us as his children. You cannot out sin the grace of God.

Capturing God

Perhaps there is no greater sin than trying to manipulate God. There is also nothing so dangerous. The Philistines capture the Ark of the Covenant in battle. They thought they now controlled Israel's God! They place the Ark in the temple of their god Dagon, only to find that Dagon bows before the Ark. The Philistines move the Ark from town to town because tumors break out in every town that holds the Ark.

Finally, the Philistines decide to send the Ark back to Israel, but they are afraid to send it back without a guilt offering. They therefore make gold images of the rats and the tumors that plague them. They send the images as a guilt offering for their sins. "Make models of the tumors and of the rats that are destroying the country, and pay honor to Israel's god. Perhaps he will lift his hand from you and your gods and your land" (1 Samuel 6:5).

Although the word "prayer" is not used here, obviously the Philistines are making supplication to the Lord. They pay honor to him. He hears. He answers. He heals them of their plagues.

This is one of the stranger stories of the Bible. It may seem far removed from our experience. We are not pagan Philistines. We have not, would not, and cannot capture the Ark of the Covenant. But we do at times act as if we control God. We say things like, "God cannot do that." "He doesn't work that way." We act as if we have figured God out. We domesticate and tame him. But he refuses to fit in our comfortable categories. We dare not box-in God!

When we catch ourselves trying to control God through our prayers, our good deeds, or our moral lives, then we must repent. We do not send golden rats and tumors to God, but we do pay honor to him. We acknowledge that no price can pay for our pride and our sin. No price but the one God himself paid in Christ.

Rejecting God's Rule

We might not try to control God, but we might want to do things God's way *and* our way. So it was with Israel. They ask God for a king so they can be like other nations. At first, that might seem insignificant. But in reality Israel was rejecting the Lord as their only king.

It took a while for Israel to realize the enormity of that rejection. Only the prophet Samuel could help them realize what they had done. When they do, they pray for forgiveness. "The people all said to Samuel, 'Pray to the Lord your God for your servants so that we will not die, for we have added to all our other sins the evil of asking for a king'" (1 Samuel 12:19).

Again, this sin may seem far removed from our experience. We Americans rejected all kings long ago! But the question for us is the same as it was for Israel. Will God alone rule in our lives? Are we content for him to be our only

Lord and Leader? Or do we think we can live like those around us, looking to other leaders—government, business, "experts," preachers—instead of to God alone? In other words, do we think the "rules" are different at work than they are in church?

If so, we too need to pray that we serve only one King. We need to pray that his kingdom will triumph. That his will be done on earth as in heaven.

The Sin of Assessment

Another strange Bible story confronts us. David the king decides to have a census to find how many fighting men he can count on when war comes. It seems like common sense. Surely any responsible nation needs to know the size of its armed forces.

But Israel is not to be like the other nations. The Lord is their king. Their trust should be in him, not in their security forces. David shows a lack of faith in God by numbering his army. As a result, God punishes not David, but the entire nation. "How unfair!" we might say from a contemporary perspective. But in Israel the king represented, even embodied the nation. David's loss of trust in God alone to give security reflected the nation's loss of confidence. David quickly realized the serious-ness of his distrust.

> David was conscience-stricken after he had counted the fighting men, and he said to the Lord, "I have sinned greatly in what I have done. Now, O Lord, I beg you, take away the guilt of your servant. I have done a very foolish thing."
>
> Before David got up the next morning, the word of the Lord had come to Gad the prophet, David's seer: "Go and tell David, 'This is what the Lord says: I am giving you three options. Choose one of them for me to carry out against you.'" So Gad went to David and said to him, "Shall there come upon you three years of famine in your land? Or three months of fleeing from your enemies while they pursue you? Or three days of plague in your land? Now then, think it over and decide how I should answer the one who sent me."
>
> David said to Gad, "I am in deep distress. Let us fall into the hands of the Lord, for his mercy is great; but do not let me fall into the hands of men."

So the Lord sent a plague on Israel from that morning until the end of the time designated, and seventy thousand of the people from Dan to Beersheba died. When the angel stretched out his hand to destroy Jerusalem, the Lord was grieved because of the calamity and said to the angel who was afflicting the people, "Enough! Withdraw your hand." The angel of the Lord was then at the threshing floor of Araunah the Jebusite.

When David saw the angel who was striking down the people, he said to the Lord, "I am the one who has sinned and done wrong. These are but sheep. What have they done? Let your hand fall upon me and my family." (2 Samuel 24:10-17)

It is unusual for God to give David a choice of punishment. Perhaps this was a test from God, to see if David had learned his lesson. He had. Even in punishment, he trusts the hand of the Lord, not human hands. If only he had trusted the Lord's hands to protect him, instead of counting his men in arms!

What can we learn about prayer from such a story? We are not kings. We do not initiate the census.

Yet we do face the perpetual question of trust. Do we trust God to protect us? Or do we (like David) think we can trust him yet place our confidence in what we can count—security forces, net worth, years of experience. It is no easier for us to trust God alone than it was for David. One sign of lacking that trust is to be constantly assessing how well we are doing professionally, economically, and even spiritually. When we realize our foolishness, then (like David) we confess and place ourselves in the hands of a God whose mercy is great.

This story has a great deal to say to those worried about shrinking churches. The numbers look grim. Overall church attendance is down. Our particular group may have lost thousands of members. Our local church is reduced to a handful. Is it time to wring our hands? To panic? To find some scheme to increase our numbers? No! It is time for audacious faithfulness and trust. God has not and will not abandon his people! We must trust his mercy when the numbers are great and when they are small.

Doing the Best We Can

What happens when you trust God, do the best you can to obey him, and still get things wrong? Do we have a God of "fine print" and technicalities who is out to get us? Or do we serve a God of love who understands the hearts of his children?

These are the questions facing King Hezekiah and Israel. For many years God's people had neglected to keep the Passover. They had even allowed God's temple to become disused and defiled. Hezekiah begins a reform that cleanses the temple, offers sacrifices, and celebrates the Passover.

However, since they had not kept the Passover in their lifetime, some of the people do not ritually cleanse themselves before participating. This is against God's law!

> Although most of the many people who came from Ephraim, Manasseh, Issachar and Zebulun had not purified themselves, yet they ate the Passover, contrary to what was written. But Hezekiah prayed for them, saying, "May the Lord, who is good, pardon everyone who sets his heart on seeking God— the Lord, the God of his fathers—even if he is not clean according to the rules of the sanctuary." And the Lord heard Hezekiah and healed the people. (2 Chronicles 30:18-20)

Even when we ignorantly break God's law, we should ask for forgiveness. However, notice that God is not a God of picky technicalities. He looks on the heart. He pardons everyone who sets their heart on seeking him.

What does this say to our lives and our prayers? It is not an invitation to laziness, ignorance, or disobedience. It is a reminder of the goodness of our God. He knows our hearts. He knows when we are sincerely seeking him. What is more, he honors those sincere attempts, feeble though they may be. The Lord hears those who approach him from the heart.

Reversing Reform

Contrast Hezekiah's heartfelt reforms with the actions of his son, Manasseh. He rebuilds the pagan altars his father had destroyed. He even places a pagan image in the temple. What's more, "He sacrificed his sons in the fire in the Valley of Ben Hinnom, practiced sorcery, divination and witchcraft, and consulted mediums and spiritists. He did much evil in the eyes of the Lord, provoking him to anger" (2 Chronicles 33:6).

In his righteous anger, God has Israel conquered and Manasseh taken to Babylon as a prisoner in chains. But that is not the end of the story. "In his distress he sought the favor of the Lord his God and humbled himself greatly before the God of his fathers. And when he prayed to him, the Lord was moved by his entreaty and listened to his plea; so he brought him back to Jerusalem and to his kingdom. Then Manasseh knew that the Lord is God." (2 Chronicles 33:12-13)

How can God forgive someone who led his own people into idol worship and child sacrifice? Can Manasseh claim ignorance? No! His father taught him better. Yet God is so merciful, he will even forgive those in open rebellion to him, if only they humbly seek him. No sin is beyond the grace of God.

Manasseh then knows that the Lord is God. How does he know? Certainly because of the Lord's power in punishing Manasseh. But more, he knows the Lord is God because of the depth of his mercy.

How do we experience the reality of God? Certainly when we witness his power. But even more so when we receive his grace. He brings us home when we do not deserve it.

Active Repentance in Prayer

Manasseh's exile to Babylon is brief. Later, God exiles most of Judah there for over sixty years. A remnant returns under the leadership of Ezra. Upon returning, Ezra first proclaims a fast, then purifies the people and offers sacrifices.

Part of that purification is to honestly confess the sins of God's people, both past and present, in a lengthy prayer (Ezra 9:5-10:3). Ezra begins the prayer by admitting the sins of their ancestors.

> Then, at the evening sacrifice, I rose from my self-abasement, with my tunic and cloak torn, and fell on my knees with my hands spread out to the Lord my God and prayed:
>
> "O my God, I am too ashamed and disgraced to lift up my face to you, my God, because our sins are higher than our heads and our guilt has reached to the heavens. From the days of our forefathers until now, our guilt has been great. Because of our sins, we and our kings and our priests have been subjected to the sword and captivity, to pillage and humiliation at the hand of foreign kings, as it is today.
>
> "But now, for a brief moment, the Lord our God has been gracious in leaving us a remnant and giving us a firm place in his sanctuary, and so

our God gives light to our eyes and a little relief in our bondage. Though we are slaves, our God has not deserted us in our bondage. He has shown us kindness in the sight of the kings of Persia: He has granted us new life to rebuild the house of our God and repair its ruins, and he has given us a wall of protection in Judah and Jerusalem. (Ezra 9:5-9)

Although God has been merciful to them, these returned exiles have sinned by intermarrying with the nations around them. Ezra confesses this on behalf of his people. The people themselves respond with vows to put away their foreign wives (see Ezra 10:1-17).

Here is a prayer that calls for action. Repentance is more than heart-felt acknowledgement of sin. It also demands a difficult response. We must stop the sinful action! In this case that meant a painful breaking up of families.

What we learn from this story is that asking for forgiveness is more than saying we are sorry. It means turning our lives over to God completely. It means removing any barrier that stands between us and God. It may even mean separating ourselves from those we love.

God's love is strong. Strong enough to forgive any sin. But that strong love demands all that we are and have. God will not tolerate any rival.

Confession and Action

Although blessed to return to Jerusalem, the remnant under the leadership of Ezra faces a difficult situation. The gates and walls of Jerusalem are in ruins. That situation is reported to Nehemiah who reacts, not with mere sympathy, but with prayer and action.

When I heard these things, I sat down and wept. For some days I mourned and fasted and prayed before the God of heaven. Then I said:

"O Lord, God of heaven, the great and awesome God, who keeps his covenant of love with those who love him and obey his commands, let your ear be attentive and your eyes open to hear the prayer your servant is praying before you day and night for your servants, the people of Israel. I confess the sins we Israelites, including myself and my father's house, have committed against you. We have acted very wickedly toward you. We have not obeyed the commands, decrees and laws you gave your servant Moses.

"Remember the instruction you gave your servant Moses, saying, 'If you are unfaithful, I will scatter you among the nations, but if you return to me and obey my commands, then even if your exiled people are at the farthest horizon, I will gather them from there and bring them to the place I have chosen as a dwelling for my Name.'

"They are your servants and your people, whom you redeemed by your great strength and your mighty hand. O Lord, let your ear be attentive to the prayer of this your servant and to the prayer of your servants who delight in revering your name. Give your servant success today by granting him favor in the presence of this man."

I was cupbearer to the king. (Nehemiah 1:4-10)

Nehemiah wishes to take more Jews to Jerusalem to rebuild its walls. However, he is not so arrogant that he thinks they deserve to return. He confesses their sin and God's justice in punishing them. But he reminds God of his promise of grace and restoration.

He also knows he cannot accomplish this task on his own. He has a trusted position, cupbearer to king Artaxerxes, but he knows he cannot go to Jerusalem without the king's permission and help.

But Nehemiah knows more. He does not rush into the king's presence, but goes into the presence of the real power behind all thrones. He asks God to give him success with the king. God hears his prayer. The king sends Nehemiah on his way with supplies, safe-conduct, and soldiers.

Like Ezra, Nehemiah learns that confession and repentance requires action. In this case, not just ending sinful practices, but actively doing the will of God. In faith, Nehemiah travels, leads, and rebuilds. Accepting the gracious forgiveness of God always leads to faithful and joyous work.

Questions for Further Discussion

1. What are some ways we try to "capture" and control God? Why do we do this? How can we keep prayer itself from being an attempt to control God?

2. Is God our king? Do we pray to him that way? If so, what does it mean to make him the only king of our lives? What rivals might he have as our king?

3. Is it comforting or frightening to know that God looks on our hearts, not merely on our outward actions?

4. Are there sins that are beyond God's grace? If not, what would keep God from forgiving us and others from sin? Are all sins forgiven?

5. Should confession and repentance always lead to action? If so, how is this different from earning our forgiveness through right action?

Try This Week

What is the one sin you seem to repeatedly commit? Focus on that sin this week. Honestly bring it to God in repentance when you pray. Accept God's forgiveness and strength.

A Book to Read

An older, out-of-print work that focuses on the relevance of Old Testament prayers for current faith is Clarence Edward Macartney, *Wrestlers with God: Prayers of the Old Testament* (Grand Rapids; Baker, 1963).

PART THREE

PRAYING
WITH THE PSALMS,
WISDOM BOOKS,
AND PROPHETS

Chapter 7

"SING ABOUT THE LORD'S WAYS"
Prayer as Songs of Struggle and Joy

May they sing of the ways of the Lord,
for the glory of the Lord is great.

PSALM 138:5

Hundreds of books have been written on the Psalms, the prayer book of the Bible. In three brief chapters we will not look at all the Psalms, but will give a taste of several types of prayers found there. That taste should increase our appetite for discovering this marvelous collection of prayer hymns.

Perhaps, like me, you did not grow up enjoying the Psalms. As a young Christian, I was taught to read through the Bible from Genesis to Revelation. But when I got to the Psalms, the "chapters" did not make sense. Psalm 1 did not logically lead to Psalm 2. There was no sequence to the reading. Moreover, there was little doctrine and instruction in the Psalms. Indeed, they sounded more like human words to God than like God's words to us.

It wasn't until later that I realized the nature of the Psalms. They are indeed human words to God, but no less inspired than the rest of the Bible. The Psalms are heartfelt prayers to God. What's more, they are poetry. Hebrew poetry is not like English poetry. It seldom relies on rhyme or rhythm. Instead, Hebrew poetry is based on parallel thoughts or feelings. In other words, genuine emotion is expressed in different words in the lines of the Psalm. Sometimes the feelings are similar in the next line, sometimes opposite, sometimes additional.

This means the Psalms are poetry put to music. As poetry, the Psalms contain metaphors, exaggeration, and other figurative and expressive language. That's why we find so little that is doctrinal (as we usually define it) in the Psalms. Of course, the Psalms are doctrinal in that they teach, but they teach as poetical prayers. Prayer may have doctrinal implications, but we rarely express doctrine in prayer. Instead, we open our hearts to God, in strong emotive language.

The Psalms are thus most like a hymnbook. Reading through the Psalms in order, trying to find a common theme, is like singing through the hymnbook in order expecting one hymn to naturally lead to another. It does not work that way. Instead, we chose hymns and psalms that best express what we feel at the moment. Thus, the best way to pray the Psalms is to begin with the question, "How do I feel toward God at the moment?" then find a psalm that best expresses that meaning.

Crying Out to the Lord

Sometimes we do not have warm feelings toward God. We might even feel disappointed and angry at him. Our child dies. Painful illness strikes us. We lose our job. Our marriage breaks up. Or in the day-to-day sameness of life we feel hopeless. Where is God? Why doesn't he do something? Why does he leave us on our own?

We might be tempted to deny these feelings of anger and disappointment with God. They don't sound like faithfulness! Yet the Psalms frequently contain honest expressions of pain in the presence of God. These faithful cries of hurt and anger are part of the Bible. God wants us to be honest with him. He is big enough to take it. Telling him that we feel abandoned by him is not breaking relationship with God. It is faithful lament.

Laments generally follow a pattern (as do many songs and psalms). We see that pattern in Psalm 142. First, the psalmist addresses God with intensity, fervently trusting that he will hear:

I cry aloud to the Lord;
I lift up my voice to the Lord for mercy.

Then the sufferer dares to cry out in honest complaint:
I pour out my complaint before him;
> before him I tell my trouble.
When my spirit grows faint within me,
> it is you who know my way.
> In the path where I walk
> men have hidden a snare for me.
Look to my right and see;
> no one is concerned for me.
> I have no refuge;
> no one cares for my life.

There is no hesitation here in telling God how we feel. Is someone out to get us? Have they hidden a snare for us? This is not paranoia, but the reality many of us face at work, at school, perhaps even at home. What do we do in the face of overwhelming odds? We appeal to the Lord. "No one cares for me." Surely we have all felt that. What do we do when we feel abandoned? We tell the Lord.

Even though complaint is the heart of a lament, there is always a turn to trust, deliverance, and assurance. We cry out to God because we believe he hears! Some of us pray about our troubles but still believe we can make things better by worrying over them. The Psalms teach us to take our problems to God and leave them there, knowing that he cares. So this psalm expresses the sure hope of deliverance.

I cry to you, O Lord;
> I say, "You are my refuge,
> my portion in the land of the living."
Listen to my cry,
> for I am in desperate need;
> rescue me from those who pursue me,
> for they are too strong for me.

We cry out in our desperate need, but we cry to one who is able and willing to listen and to rescue. That is why laments that begin with shocking words of complaint usually end with words of praise.

Set me free from my prison,
> that I may praise your name.
Then the righteous will gather about me
> because of your goodness to me.

Psalm 142 is just one example of lament in the Psalms. For others, read Psalms 3, 12, 22, 31, 39, 42, 44, 57, 71, 80, 94, 120, 137, and 139. When our distress is so great that we do not know how to pray, these psalms help us to open our broken hearts to the only One who will listen, act, and heal. Jesus himself uses the words of a lament psalm to express his deepest agony.

My God, my God, why have you forsaken me?
> Why are you so far from saving me,
> so far from the words of my groaning?
> > (Psalm 22:1)

If the Son of God hanging on the cross could faithfully complain to God in lament, then we too can keep faith and yet be honest to God. He is a God who wants to hear our cry.

Giving Thanks

It may seem like an abrupt move from complaining in lament to thanking God for his blessings. Yet in structure, we see many of the same movements in both types of Psalms. Thanksgiving Psalms are what we pray when the trouble is past. Our pain seemed too great, our obstacles too powerful to overcome. But we took our troubles to God. He heard. He acted. Now, we look back on how God powerfully delivered us from evil. And we give thanks.

Thanksgiving Psalms usually begin with a statement of praise, as in Psalm 138:

I will praise you, O Lord, with all my heart;
> before the "gods" I will sing your praise.
I will bow down toward your holy temple
> and will praise your name
> > for your love and your faithfulness,

for you have exalted above all things
>your name and your word.

After praising God, the psalmist recalls God's deliverance:

When I called, you answered me;
>you made me bold and stouthearted.

In light of God's deliverance, the psalmist then calls on others to give praise to God for what he has done. This shows that the Psalms, although deeply personal, are not private. They draw others into relationship with a giving God:

May all the kings of the earth praise you, O Lord,
>when they hear the words of your mouth.
May they sing of the ways of the Lord,
>for the glory of the Lord is great.

Then the psalmist confesses that God will continue to deliver from trouble:

Though the Lord is on high, he looks upon the lowly,
>but the proud he knows from afar.
Though I walk in the midst of trouble,
>you preserve my life;
>you stretch out your hand against the anger of my foes,
>with your right hand you save me.

Finally, Psalm 138 ends with personal testimony to God's faithfulness:

The Lord will fulfill his purpose for me;
>your love, O Lord, endures forever—
>do not abandon the works of your hands.

Other thanksgiving psalms (18, 30, 32, 34, 40, 65, 66, 67, 75, 92, 107, 116, 118, 124, 136) generally follow this sequence of praise, remembered distress, appeal to others to give thanks, remembered deliverance, and personal testimony of faith. These thanksgiving psalms can serve today as guides for personal and communal expressions of gratitude to God.

I have a busy friend who could not find much time for prayer. She decided simply to turn off the radio and phone when she was driving and spend that time counting her blessings. It shapes her whole day. In those times, the words of gratitude found in the Psalms come alive for her. Count your blessings! Give thanks to God!

Songs of Praise

Praise to God looks much like giving thanks. The distinction between them is that generally in thanksgiving psalms we praise God for what he has done. He has blessed. He has delivered. In praise psalms we recognize the greatness of God himself. We praise him simply for who he is, not just what he has done for us. This is not an absolute distinction. Praise psalms often mention the works of God and thanksgiving psalms sometimes praise him merely for his nature.

Yet it is important to remember that God would be worthy of praise even if he had never done anything for us. His very nature deserves praise! But how much more do we praise him when we realize how much he cares for us. This is why so many Old Testament figures pray with hands raised to God. They praise him with their bodies!

As an example of a praise psalm, consider Psalm 100, sung in many forms by believers throughout the ages:

Shout for joy to the Lord, all the earth.
Worship the Lord with gladness;
    come before him with joyful songs.
Know that the Lord is God.
    It is he who made us, and we are his;
    we are his people, the sheep of his pasture.
Enter his gates with thanksgiving
    and his courts with praise;
     give thanks to him and praise his name.
For the Lord is good and his love endures forever;
    his faithfulness continues through all generations.

Here in praise we confess that the Lord alone is God. We praise him for being the Creator. We praise him for his goodness and love. At the center of every prayer we pray—request, intercession, confession, or lament—is recognition of the praiseworthy

God to whom we pray. Praise is the language of prayer. The praise psalms (8, 19, 33, 66, 100, 103, 104, 111, 113, 114, 117, 145, 146, 147, 149) instruct us in that language. That is why these psalms, more than others, have been paraphrased into hymns and songs of praise. When we catch a glimpse of the Almighty and All-loving God, we cannot help but break out into song. "Praise the Lord" becomes more than a cliché.

Praise the Lord, all you nations;
    extol him, all you peoples.
For great is his love toward us,
    and the faithfulness of the Lord endures forever.
    Praise the Lord. (Psalm 117)

Trusting His Love

Our confidence in the enduring love of God expresses itself in psalms of trust. These psalms face the difficulties of life head-on. Unlike the reputation we often have, God's followers do not sugar-coat the realities of life. These psalms (11, 16, 23, 27, 62, 63, 91, 121, 125, 131) graphically describe the enemies we face—war, disease, poverty, injustice, terror, and uncertainty. However, in spite of these enemies (or rather, *because* of them), the psalmist expresses trust in the Lord, who provides justice, safety, and guidance.

These are not just songs of trust but prayers of hope. Hope is not fondly wishing for things to get better. Hope is not optimism. It is not based on human planning, government programs, or mere luck. Hope springs from trust in the character of God. These Psalms speak of that hope by describing God as light (27:1), rock (62:2), fortress (91:2), shepherd (23), and even mother (131:2). He is the one who gently protects us and shows us the way.

Therefore, it is not mere protection and care we desire. Our deepest desire is for God himself. He alone can satisfy the longings of our hearts:

O God, you are my God,
    earnestly I seek you;
    my soul thirsts for you,
    my body longs for you,

in a dry and weary land
where there is no water.

(Psalm 63:1)

Here is intense desire for God, a longing we cannot put into words. All our other hungers point to this one—the thirst and hunger for relationship with God. When we are weary to our bones, we find rest in him alone (Psalm 62:1). When we view a world that is achingly beautiful, our hearts expand with the need to gaze upon the one who is Beauty:

One thing I ask of the Lord,
this is what I seek:
that I may dwell in the house of the Lord
all the days of my life,
to gaze upon the beauty of the Lord
and to seek him in his temple.

(Psalm 27:4)

Our trust is in the Lord who desires us more than we do him. In spite of disease, terror, poverty, and even death, we still believe in a God who cares, who saves, and who loves. I have a friend who stopped praying for people to get well. Everyone he prayed for got worse and died. Although it may seem that our prayers accomplish nothing, or that our troubles actually intensify after prayer, we continue to pray in faith and hope. Prayer is about relationship with God, not about immediate help. And as with all human relationships, that faith and hope is sometimes tested by circumstances. But we pray not primarily as those who seek relief from troubles, but as those who long for a loving Father.

Praying in Sorrow and Joy

What kind of week have you had? Perhaps everything has gone great. You and your family are healthy. The kids are doing well in school. You received praise and even a raise at work. What do we do in the good weeks? We give praise to God!

But what if you've had "one of those weeks"? Everything has gone wrong. Bad news from the doctor. A distressing conference with the teacher. Overdrawn at the bank. You lose your job. How can you stand Sunday in church and sing, "Praise to the Lord"?

Only by honestly bringing your problems to God in prayer. Tell him how you feel. Cry. Shout. Complain. Do all that knowing who God is. A God who cares. A God who is in control. A God who hears our cry. A God we can trust.

We cry out to God in our own words. Yet sometimes we cannot find the words. That is why the Psalms are so helpful. By daily saying these psalms of lament, thanksgiving, and praise, these words become our own. They both shape and express the deepest feelings of our hearts.

Questions for Further Discussion

1. Do you naturally express your feelings in poems and songs? How does your answer affect your attitude toward the Psalms?

2. Do we sometimes hesitate to complain before God? If so, why? Should we overcome that hesitation?

3. Why do laments usually end in praise? Is this simply making the best of a bad situation? How can we honestly praise God when we are complaining to him?

4. What are you thankful for? What do you take for granted and forget to be thankful for? How can the Psalms help us give thanks?

5. What first comes to mind when you hear the word "praise"? Why should we give praise to God? Is praise an obligation or a joy?

Try This Week

Write a poem that expresses praise and thanksgiving toward God (it does not have to rhyme). Does writing or thinking in poetry help you to pray?

A Book to Read

A good book by a scholar on the Psalms is Walter Brueggemann, *The Psalms and the Life of Faith* (Minneapolis: Fortress, 1995).

Chapter 8

"HOW LOVELY IS YOUR DWELLING PLACE"
Prayer as Songs of Celebration

How lovely is your dwelling place,
O Lord Almighty!
My soul yearns, even faints, for the courts of the Lord;
my heart and my flesh cry out for the living God.

PSALM 84:1-2

While most of the Psalms are hymns of lament, praise, thanksgiving, and trust, many are special occasion psalms. We know what it is like at church when we focus on special times. Funeral hymns are not appropriate at weddings. Songs during Lent are different than those at Easter. We do not go Christmas caroling in July.

So also in ancient Israel. Certain psalms were associated with particular times of celebration. By looking at these psalms, we too can learn how to relate to God in those special moments of life.

God Renews Covenant

Out of his great love, God led his people out of slavery in Egypt. He brought them to Mt. Sinai where he made a solemn covenant with them. "Covenant" is a word we do not use often. Perhaps the closest we get to the experience is when we make solemn vows to one another in marriage. At the heart of covenant is relationship. Dedicated, committed, exclusive relationship bound by unbreakable promises. So it was with God and Israel. God initiated the covenant, promising to be the Israelites' God and to bless them. The people responded with a vow to be faithful and obedient to God: "When Moses went and told the people all the Lord's words and laws, they responded with one voice, 'Everything the Lord has said we will do'" (Exodus 24:3). Moses then sprinkles the people with blood, symbolizing the seriousness of their promise.

This deeply moving covenant renewal ceremony was to be repeated every seven years in Israel, reminding each generation of the amazing blessings and profound responsibilities of being God's people (see Deuteronomy 31:9-13). It is not clear whether Israel kept this ritual every seven years, but we do know of occasions where the whole nation gathered to renew their vows to the Lord (see Joshua 8:30-35, 24:1-28; 1 Samuel 11:14-12:25; 2 Kings 23:1-3; 1 Chronicles 28:1-21; 2 Chronicles 29:1-33; Nehemiah 8:1-12).

On those occasions of covenant renewal, the people broke out in songs that expressed their conflicted hearts. One the one hand, they faced the Almighty knowing that they had not been faithful to their covenant vows. Part of renewing the covenant was honest repentance and a pledge to sincere obedience. Psalm 50 says it is a frightening thing to break covenant with God!

> Our God comes and will not be silent;
>> a fire devours before him,
>> and around him a tempest rages.
> He summons the heavens above,
>> and the earth, that he may judge his people:
> "Gather to me my consecrated ones,
>> who made a covenant with me by sacrifice."
> And the heavens proclaim his righteousness,
>> for God himself is judge. (Psalm 50:3-6)

In Psalm 50, God goes on to condemn his people for offering sacrifices without keeping their vows of obedience.

This seems like a strange song to sing. What a downer! We sing of a God who judges our disobedience. But we cannot renew our covenant with God without taking seriously our failures to keep covenant. And if we turn back to God, he graciously forgives. So the psalm ends with these words from a loving God:

> He who sacrifices thank offerings honors me,
> > and he prepares the way
> > so that I may show him the salvation of God.
>
> (Psalm 50:23)

Thus, covenant renewal begins in the sorrow of repentance but ends with the joy of salvation. That joyful experience of covenant renewal is sung out in Psalm 81:

> Sing for joy to God our strength;
> > shout aloud to the God of Jacob!
> Begin the music, strike the tambourine,
> > play the melodious harp and lyre.
> Sound the ram's horn at the New Moon,
> > and when the moon is full, on the day of our Feast;
> this is a decree for Israel,
> > an ordinance of the God of Jacob. (Psalm 81:1-4)

This Psalm continues with the story of God delivering his people from slavery and preserving them in the wilderness. Our God maintains his relationship with us in spite of our failures. We can only respond to such grace with shouting and singing with overwhelming joy.

How do we sing these songs and pray these prayers today? Don't we as God's people need to set aside times to pledge anew our loyalty to God?

Indeed we do. One place we do this is at the table of the Lord. The Lord's Supper is a covenant meal. When Jesus took the cup at the last Supper, he said, "This cup is the new covenant in my blood, which is poured out for you" (Luke 22:20). That's why the hymns we sing and the prayers we pray around the Supper sound so much like these two psalms. We pour out our heartfelt sorrow at breaking covenant with God. We confess that we have done things we should not and left undone things we should do.

But the Supper as covenant renewal is also celebration. We sing and shout for God is our strength. He has led. He has redeemed. He has given himself for us. Perhaps it would help us to use these psalms around the Supper to remind us that here we renew our vows to God in solemnity and in joy.

God Is Our King

There were special occasions when Israel gave praise to her king. One was when a new king was crowned. Much like our inauguration day, this was a time for celebration and psalm. Like all nations, Israel also praised her kings after victory in battle.

Such praise might strike us as mere patriotism. But these times of glory for the king were much more than Israel's version of the Fourth of July or the pledge to the flag. Israel was not like other nations. Her king was not simply a human ruler alongside others. He was the anointed one of God. He was God's representative on earth. However, Israel was not to think too highly of the king. Although he was king by divine right, that meant all of his power and authority rested in God, not himself. In other words, the Lord alone was the true king of Israel.

That truth is made clear in what are called the royal psalms. They do not praise the king for his accomplishments, but they praise God for blessing the king. These psalms are prayers for God's continued goodness toward the king and the nation.

> O Lord, the king rejoices in your strength.
>> How great is his joy in the victories you give!
> You have granted him the desire of his heart
>> and have not withheld the request of his lips.
>> Selah
> You welcomed him with rich blessings
>> and placed a crown of pure gold on his head.
> He asked you for life, and you gave it to him—
>> length of days, for ever and ever.
> Through the victories you gave, his glory is great;
>> you have bestowed on him splendor and majesty.
> Surely you have granted him eternal blessings
>> and made him glad with the joy of your presence.

For the king trusts in the Lord;

> through the unfailing love of the Most High
>
> he will not be shaken. (Psalm 21:1-7)

This and other royal psalms (18, 20, 45, 72, 101, 110, 144) proclaim that victory and prosperity come from God alone. The king and the nation receive these gifts by faith, not by their own brilliance or power. In the Old Testament what makes one a good king or a bad king is not prowess in battle or cleverness in administration. A good king trusts God alone. A bad king puts his trust in himself, in others, or in strange gods.

The intimate relationship between God and the king is expressed by the word "anointed." Anointing with oil was more than a ritual that made one king. It was anointing with the power of God. That is why "anointed one" ("Messiah" in Hebrew, "Christ" in Greek) was such a powerful term in both the Old and the New Testaments. It also explains why two royal psalms (2, 110) are the most quoted in the New Testament.

Why do the nations conspire and the peoples plot in vain?

The kings of the earth take their stand

> and the rulers gather together against the Lord
>
> and against his Anointed One.

"Let us break their chains," they say,

> "and throw off their fetters."

The One enthroned in heaven laughs;

> the Lord scoffs at them.

Then he rebukes them in his anger

> and terrifies them in his wrath, saying,

"I have installed my King

> on Zion, my holy hill."

I will proclaim the decree of the Lord:

> He said to me, "You are my Son;
>
> today I have become your Father. (Psalm 2:1-7)

No wonder that when early Christians read "his Anointed One" and "You are my Son" they thought immediately of their experience with Jesus of Nazareth. However, it is important to remember that these words in their original context of Israel referred to the king. God thought so highly of Israel's king, he calls him "son." Thus the words the Israelites sang to praise their king are sung by Christians to praise theirs.

For the New Testament writers, the most provocative phrase in the royals psalms is this:

> The Lord says to my Lord:
>> "Sit at my right hand
>> until I make your enemies
>> a footstool for your feet." (Psalm 110:1)

Several speakers in the New Testament (see Luke 20:43, Acts 2:35, Hebrews 1:13), understand "my Lord" to refer to Jesus as the victorious king over all his enemies. This again shows how the royal psalms shape Christian worship.

In a democratic age where monarchs are either powerless figureheads or considered tyrannical despots, it is difficult to appreciate psalms that praise the king. However, we must remember that the church is not a democracy but an absolute monarchy. These psalms can remind us that God through Christ reigns in our lives. We dare not put our trust in any other power or ruler, not even a democratically elected one. That's why there are another group of psalms that describe not the king, but the Lord God enthroned in glory (Psalms 24, 29, 47, 93, 95, 96, 97, 98, 99). Him alone we praise:

> Sing praises to God, sing praises;
>> sing praises to our King, sing praises.
> For God is the King of all the earth;
>> sing to him a psalm of praise. (Psalm 47:6-7)

How can the contemporary church recover these psalms? What if we used one of the patriotic days on our calendars (President's Day, the Fourth of July, Veterans' Day) to remind ourselves that our true ruler is the Lord God? A worship time based on these psalms could help us keep our patriotism in a healthy perspective. The Lord is King!

The Presence of God

As we saw in an earlier chapter, when Solomon dedicates the temple he clearly states that no building can contain God. Having said that, it is still true that the presence of God (usually called the "glory of the Lord") was intensively in the temple. The Israelites came to Jerusalem, to the temple on Mount Zion, to worship, sacrifice, and pray.

Thus, there are psalms—Songs of Zion—that rejoice in the special experience of God's presence in the temple. These psalms (46, 48, 76, 84, 87, 122) refer to Zion, Jerusalem, the courts of God, and the house of God as places where a joyous encounter with the Lord takes place.

> How lovely is your dwelling place,
>> O Lord Almighty!
> My soul yearns, even faints,
>> for the courts of the Lord;
>> my heart and my flesh cry out
>> for the living God. (Psalm 84:1-2)

These words capture the deep hunger for God. In a world at worst threatening and at best ordinary, we long for a place where we can encounter the living and loving God. For Israel, the temple was that place.

> Within your temple, O God,
>> we meditate on your unfailing love. (Psalm 48:9)

Where do we find God today? Where is the place we experience his presence? No doubt there are locations special to us and to others. These "thin places" where the boundaries between heaven and earth fade show us the need for special places of prayer. Jesus himself preferred mountains. Perhaps you have such a place, maybe just a corner of a room, where you regularly meditate on the love of God.

But the primary temple of God today is in the human heart. We are the temple of God. These psalms can help us express the profound hunger we feel for God's presence. Our hearts and flesh cry out for him. They voice the prayer of all believers, that God will live in us and we in him. No matter where we are, these psalms can serve as guides to meditation on the unfailing love of God.

God's Enduring Love

We know the outline of the story of God's love. God creates the world. He fashions humanity in his image. Humans turn from God. God in his mercy redeems through

Abraham and his descendents. That redemption reaches a climax in the Exodus and in the covenant at Sinai. Yet in spite of God's unfailing love, the Israelites grumble in the wilderness. They turn to other gods. Even when God leads them to the Promised Land, they will not serve him exclusively. But in the face of their rejection, God's love remains. He longs for his people to return to him so he can bless them.

It is this story of God's redemptive love that is celebrated in some of the Psalms, called salvation history psalms. They recount this story not as ancient history, but as the story God's people should embrace. It is their story. Their lives draw meaning from the acts of God. It is our story. Not just interesting (or boring) biblical history, but the story that shapes our lives and gives us our identity. We are the people of God, a God who loves forever. As God's people, we break forth in praise and prayer to our ever-loving, infinitely-patient Father.

For example, Psalm 105 gives thanks to God for what he has done through Abraham, Isaac, Jacob, Joseph, Moses, and Aaron. It recounts the Exodus and the conquest of the land of Canaan as examples of God's faithfulness. It tells the story of a God who is dependable:

> For he remembered his holy promise
>> given to his servant Abraham.
> He brought out his people with rejoicing,
>> his chosen ones with shouts of joy;
> he gave them the lands of the nations,
>> and they fell heir to what others had toiled for-
> that they might keep his precepts
>> and observe his laws.
>> Praise the Lord. (Psalm 105:42-45)

Again, this is no mere history lesson. These are more than names to be learned. More than heroes of the Bible. These people trusted the promises of God when those promises were hard to believe. These psalms show that there is only one hero in the Bible. God alone makes the promises come true.

Some trust the promises of God. Some do not. While God is always faithful, his people often put their trust in other gods. The salvation history psalms tell that part of the story, too. Although God delivers his people from slavery in Egypt, "they soon forgot what he had done" (Psalm 106:13). These psalms correct this amnesia by reminding God's people that idols can do nothing to save them (see Psalm 135:15-18).

These psalms remind us that we walk backward into the future. We cannot easily see where we are going when we walk backward. In the same way, our view of the future is unclear. What we can see is how God has been faithful to us in the past. By recounting God's deliverance in the past, these psalms encourage trust in his future love. For example, Psalm 136 tells the story of God's work from the creation through the conquest, with the repeated refrain, "His love endures forever."

As we look back at our own lives, we clearly see times where God has saved us from what seemed like impossible situations. As we face the future (or back into it), we enter it with confidence, knowing that the God who loved in our past is the God whose love forever endures. What a song to sing! What a prayer to pray!

Questions for Further Discussion

1. Compare baptism, where we enter into covenant with God, with the Lord's Supper, where we renew that covenant. How are these times like Israel's covenant renewal ceremonies? What are some specific themes in the Psalms that are relevant to baptism and the Supper?

2. What first comes to mind when you hear "king"? Are there negative thoughts we need to overcome when we think of God as king?

3. Who is the ultimate ruler over all earthly political powers? How do we show political leaders that they do not have ultimate authority? Should Christians be completely loyal and patriotic to the country in which they live?

4. Where do you go to find God? Where do you especially feel his presence?

5. What is your story of how God has loved you? How does it fit into the larger story of God's love for Israel?

Try This Week

Think of special occasions in your family (birthdays, anniversaries, holidays). Chose one and find an appropriate psalm for that occasion. Use the psalm as a way to make that day dedicated to God.

A Book to Read

A practical guide to making the Psalms a guide to our prayers is Eugene Peterson, *Answering God: The Psalms as Tools for Prayer* (San Francisco: Harper, 1989).

CHAPTER 9

"TRUST IN THE LORD AND DO GOOD"
Prayer as Words of Wisdom

Trust in the Lord and do good;
dwell in the land and enjoy safe pasture.
Delight yourself in the Lord
and he will give you the desires of your heart.

PSALM 37:3-4

"Wisdom" is a word used seldom in our time. Indeed, it sounds old fashioned or quaint. In the Bible the word originally referred to those with special skills in building or the arts (see Exodus 28:3; 31:6; 1 Chronicles 22:15; 28:21). From there, the meaning changed to describe those skilled in the art of good living. Thus, wisdom was considered to be the highest human achievement because the wise knew how to cope with life and bring order out of chaos. Wisdom is more than "common sense," it also implies integrity.

In the Bible, wisdom begins with "the fear of the Lord." It is the gift God gives to those who ask. The gift of living life well. At the heart of biblical wisdom is trust in God. Therefore, prayer in the wisdom books reflects the struggle humans sometimes have in trusting God. In times of prosperity, that trust is easy. Our blessings come from the Lord. In times of trouble, our faith is tested.

Trusting God's Wisdom

Trusting God means we trust his governance of the world. To help us express that trust, there are psalms that focus on God's wisdom. These wisdom psalms reflect the same thoughts found in the Wisdom books of the Old Testament—Proverbs, Ecclesiastes, and Job (these books contain over half of the references to "wisdom" in the Old Testament). These psalms use the same vocabulary of those books— "wisdom," "understanding," and "proverb" (see Psalm 49). Their prayer language often expresses a firm confidence that God will punish the foolish and wicked but will reward the wise and obedient.

> Do not fret because of evil men
>> or be envious of those who do wrong;
> for like the grass they will soon wither,
>> like green plants they will soon die away.
> Trust in the Lord and do good;
>> dwell in the land and enjoy safe pasture.
> Delight yourself in the Lord
>> and he will give you the desires of your heart. (Psalm 37:1-4)

God will ultimately bring justice, although now it looks as though the evil prosper and the good suffer. The conviction that God will not hear the prayers of the wicked reflects trust in God's justice.

> If anyone turns a deaf ear to the law,
>> even his prayers are detestable. (Proverbs 28:9)

Does God hear the prayer of sinners? We certainly hope so! We are all sinners before God. But does he hear those who refuse to obey him? Does he bless those who pray to him, but have no intention of making him their Lord? Of course not. Otherwise, prayer would become magic or superstition. It would be saying the right words to get God in our power, instead of falling on our face humbly before our Maker. Prayer is all about relationship with God, not about trying to manipulate him.

God detests the prayers of those who merely play at relationship with him and do not take him seriously. But he is always willing to hear those who honestly pray.

Genuinely seeking God is called "the fear of the Lord" in the wisdom literature. God always blesses those seekers:

> Blessed are all who fear the Lord,
> > who walk in his ways. (Psalm 128:1)
> Praise the Lord.
> > Blessed is the man who fears the Lord,
> > who finds great delight in his commands. (Psalm 112:1)

These Psalms go on to list the blessings God gives to those who seek him—children, wealth, security, and long life. He hears and delights in their prayers (Proverbs 15:8, 29). What a great encouragement to pray! We serve a God who gives good gifts. We have a loving Father who wants to provide all that we need. All we need to do is ask!

Questioning God's Wisdom

But is it really that simple? Doesn't that sound too easy? Do we not know those who ask and do not receive? Have we not agonized in prayer and sometimes not received a blessing? Why do the righteous suffer if God hears our prayers?

These questions are not new. They are faced head on by a man named Job.

God is so proud of Job that he brags about him to Satan. Satan responds that Job serves God only because God blesses Job so much. To prove Satan wrong, God allows him to take away blessings from Job. Job loses everything. Wealth. Position. Respect. Family. Even his health.

How do we pray when we have lost everything? How do we pray when prayer does not change things? How do we pray when prayer makes things worse? Why pray at all, if God does not hear?

These are the questions Job raises about prayer. At first, his reaction to his calamities is one of prayerful resignation:

> At this, Job got up and tore his robe and shaved his head. Then he fell to the ground in worship and said:
> "Naked I came from my mother's womb,
> and naked I will depart.
> The Lord gave and the Lord has taken away;
> may the name of the Lord be praised." (Job 1:20-21)

Here is an amazing prayer in time of suffering. Job risks placing himself completely in the hands of the Lord.

Soon, however, Job's three friends come and try to comfort him. At first they somewhat succeed because they sit with him, silently sharing his suffering for seven days. But then they open their mouths. They feel compelled to defend God. To defend him they feel they must condemn Job. Their view is simple. God rewards the righteous. He punishes the wicked. Therefore Job must have committed some great evil for God to send these terrible punishments upon him.

Job defends his innocence. He does not arrogantly claim to be completely sinless. But he has not done anything so terrible as to deserve this—poverty, bereavement, sickness, and shame. Job knows his heart is pure. Why then has the Lord sent these calamities? Why does God not hear his prayers?

My face is red with weeping,
> deep shadows ring my eyes;
yet my hands have been free of violence
> and my prayer is pure. (Job 16:17)

Still his "friends" persist, calling him terrible names. Job in turn describes them as miserable comforters.

Having to defend himself against those he calls friends changes Job's prayers. He begins to see that he is not alone. Others cry out to God for justice, but he does not punish their oppressors.

The groans of the dying rise from the city,
> and the souls of the wounded cry out for help.
But God charges no one with wrongdoing. (Job 24:12)

What good does it do to pray? It does not always help the oppressed. What's more, those who do not pray sometimes prosper more than those who do!

They spend their years in prosperity
> and go down to the grave in peace.
Yet they say to God, 'Leave us alone!
> We have no desire to know your ways.
Who is the Almighty, that we should serve him?
> What would we gain by praying to him?' (Job 21:13-15)

So if prayer does no good, why pray? Job does not have an answer, yet he persists in praying. He prays to God even when he is convinced God will not answer. "I cry out to you, O God, but you do not answer; I stand up, but you merely look at me" (Job 30:20). Why does Job keep praying? Is he a fool to do so? His friends think so. Are we fools to keep praying when it seems God does not answer? Many of our friends think so.

There is a profound lesson on prayer here. Prayer is not primarily about changing things. We do not pray merely to be blessed. Job indeed serves God for nothing. He persists in the relationship with God even when it seems there is nothing there for him. He prays for nothing. He prays because he has relationship with God. A dangerous God who (from Job's perspective) punishes for no reason. A God who makes the wicked prosper. A God who ignores the oppressed. A God who will not answer.

But finally God answers. He answers Job out of a whirlwind. He overwhelms Job with his power and majesty. Yet he does not answer Job's questions about justice and prayer. Instead he questions Job: "Where were you when I made the world?"

God's answer is God himself. He is God. We are not. We are not big enough to question how he runs the world.

I do not like that answer. Job may not have liked it either. But it is an answer that calls for trust. Why do we pray and nothing happens? Why do we pray and things get worse? Why do others reject prayer and receive more blessings than we do? Why doesn't God end injustice now?

The only answer we get is the answer Job got. The answer is God himself. That is enough for Job. It must be enough for us.

So why pray? Job's experience (and ours, if we are honest) shatters the easy answers of his friends. It shatters the shallow views of prayer around today. Prayer is all about relationship with God. That relationship is not always sweetness and light for us. It sometimes is bitterness and suffering. Yet, like Job, we persist in prayer because we trust God even when, especially when, we do not understand. Questioning God's wisdom can lead to a deeper faith.

The psalmist says it well in another of the wisdom psalms. Reflecting on the prosperity of the wicked, he says:

> When I tried to understand all this,
> > it was oppressive to me

till I entered the sanctuary of God;

>then I understood their final destiny. (Psalm 73:16-17)

Job's questions and our questions are swallowed up in our experience of God's presence. When we see God, we respond not with questions, but with praise. This is the essence of prayer.

Praying for the Foolish

Job's questioning prayers are not the final ones in his story. Although God does not answer Job's questions, he does praise Job and he condemns Eliphaz and Job's friends:

> "I am angry with you and your two friends, because you have not spoken of
> me what is right, as my servant Job has. So now take seven bulls and seven
> rams and go to my servant Job and sacrifice a burnt offering for yourselves.
> My servant Job will pray for you, and I will accept his prayer and not deal
> with you according to your folly. You have not spoken of me what is right,
> as my servant Job has." (Job 42:7-8)

What a turn of events! For days they have condemned Job with increasing fervor. Now they must go to Job to intercede with them in prayer.

What would we do in Job's shoes? Laugh? Tell them, "Tough luck"? Make them grovel for a while? Job simply prays for them. God accepts his prayer and forgives them.

Here is true forgiveness. Real love for enemies. Few things hurt worse than betrayal. Those we thought were friends turn against us. Yet Job prays for those who harm him. We cannot help but think of another who prayed, "Father, forgive them, they do not know what they are doing" (Luke 23:34). We remember words like, "Love your enemies and pray for those who persecute you" (Matthew 5:44).

Wise Prayer

So what do we learn about prayer from the Wisdom literature? On the one hand, those who trust God will be blessed. Those who do not will suffer. Sincere prayer is shown by genuinely following God. Those who pray with no intention to obey will not be heard. Those whose hearts are turned toward him can pray with confidence that he hears and responds.

Yet, at times it does not seem that way. At times prayer seems worthless or even counter-productive. We pray from sincere hearts. We truly want to please the Lord. We know he has blessed us in the past. We cry out to him in need, confident that he will hear.

We get no answer. Life is still unfair. We cannot find a job. Our savings disappear. Those we love sicken and die a lingering, painful death. Where is God? Why doesn't he answer?

And all the time we wait for him, we see those who laugh at God and at us prospering. Their children are happy and healthy. They have enough money to live the good life. Everything seems to come easy to them.

So what do we do? We continue to pray. Like Job, we pray when it seems prayer does no good. We pray when God does not hear. We pray when God is against us. We pray when others tell us we are fools and should curse God and die. We pray trusting in spite of appearances. We pray in hope against all hope. We pray to the God who spoke the world into being, the God too big for us. We pray and trust our little lives with God.

And what looks like foolishness to those around us, and even (at times) to ourselves, proves in the end to be wisdom. God appears. He speaks. He makes things right.

That is faithful prayer.

Questions for Further Discussion _____

1. What does the word "wisdom" mean to you? What are other words we use today for this idea?

2. If we trust God will he always give us the desires of our hearts? Does this mean we get everything we want by praying? Why or why not?

3. According to Job's friends, why doesn't God hear Job's prayers? Is their explanation correct? Why doesn't God hear our prayers?

4. Is it difficult to pray when we do not understand how God answers? Can we trust a God we do not understand? Why?

5. Are their people who have hurt you that you need to pray for? Why should you pray for them? Why does Job pray for his friends who hurt him so deeply?

Try This Week

Think of a prayer that you feel God has not answered. This week persist in that prayer, trusting that God loves you and wants to bless. At the end of the week, see if your attitude toward God has changed.

A Book to Read

Another scholarly but helpful book on Old Testament prayer is Samuel E. Ballantine, *Prayer in the Hebrew Bible: The Drama of Divine-Human Dialogue* (Minneapolis: Fortress, 1993).

CHAPTER 10

"YET I WILL REJOICE IN THE LORD"
Prayer as Dangerous Questions

Praise be to the name of God for ever and ever;
wisdom and power are his.

DANIEL 2:20

The prophets pray the same types of prayers found in the rest of the Old Testament—laments, thanksgiving, intercession, requests, and praise. However, there is an intensity in their prayers because of their circumstances. They pray in the hour of Israel's deepest need. Facing foreign armies, famine, and exile, they cry out to the Lord. Yet they pray in hope that God will turn his people's hearts toward him and deliver them from evil. By praying this way, the prophets raise questions about prayer that all God's people have asked.

Isaiah—To Whom Shall We Pray?

Isaiah the prophet lives in a time when many of God's people looked to other gods for help. He condemns this attempt as foolish. He ridicules the idea that one can take a piece of wood, use some for firewood, and then make the rest into a "god" that can save (Isaiah 40:9-20). Only self-deception will allow one to trust in such gods.

They cannot hear. They cannot save. We make them, not them us. Praying to such gods is a complete exercise in futility (see Isaiah 16:12; 45:20).

This is more than simply having the right God. It is more than knowing that the Lord alone is God. The condemnation of idolatry points to the character of the Lord and to the essence of prayer. Our God is a God who hears. Who listens. Who acts. Praying to him is not an empty ritual, as it must be with pagan gods. Instead, we pray to a loving Father who wants relationship with us. Praying to God is more of an interchange and a dialogue, rather than magic words that make him do our bidding.

How do contemporary children of God relate to Old Testament words about idolatry? It does seem so foolish to us, so far removed from our experience. Imagine someone whittling up a god, placing it on the mantle, and bowing to it! We would never consider doing such a thing.

But we do have our idols. We have those things that humans have created and have trusted. The economy. The government. Expertise. Success. Pleasure. Money. Happiness. Our own strategies to make life better. Isaiah warns us that it does no good to "pray" to these gods. They will not deliver what they promise. They only deceive.

Instead we pray to the only One who hears us and acts on our behalf. The all-powerful God who loves us more than we can fathom. The God who wants us to be with him in prayer.

But that prayer must be sincere. We must pray with our lives, not just with our lips. So Isaiah warns against trusting in prayer while ignoring and violently oppressing the powerless.

When you spread out your hands in prayer,
> I will hide my eyes from you;
> even if you offer many prayers, I will not listen.
> Your hands are full of blood;
> wash and make yourselves clean.
> Take your evil deeds out of my sight!
>
> (Isaiah 1:15-16)

It does no good to pray to the right God if we still pray like pagans, thinking prayer without right living pleases God. Prayer is all about relationship with the Lord.

But the genuineness of that relationship shows itself in having the heart of God for the poor and oppressed.

It also means having God's heart for all people, not just those like us. God promises that he will gather the scattered Israelites unto himself. But he also will gather those foreigners who bind themselves to him. Thus, prayer to God is never meant to exclude the other, the foreigner, the stranger, or even the enemy. "For my house will be called a house of prayer for all nations" (Isaiah 56:7).

To whom shall we pray? To the only true God. To the God who hears and acts. To the God who desires a give-and-take relationship with us. To the God who demands we act justly as those who call on him in prayer. To the God who invites all to bind themselves to him in prayer.

Jeremiah—For Whom Should We Pray?

Since God invites all to his house of prayer, then surely God's people should pray for everyone. It is shocking then to find that more than once God orders Jeremiah not to pray for his people (Jeremiah 7:16; 11:14; 14:11). Why? Why would anyone ever be told, "Do not pray for them"? Can we outsin God's grace? Is there a point beyond which God cannot or will not forgive?

No. God's grace is unfailing. But he cannot forgive those who refuse his forgiveness. In Jeremiah's day, God's people were doing terrible things, then expecting God to excuse their actions:

"Will you steal and murder, commit adultery and perjury, burn incense to Baal and follow other gods you have not known, and then come and stand before me in this house, which bears my Name, and say, 'We are safe'-safe to do all these detestable things? Has this house, which bears my Name, become a den of robbers to you? But I have been watching! declares the Lord." (Jeremiah 7:8-11)

No wonder God says, "Do not pray for them," that is, "Do not pray that they be forgiven without changing and turning to me." God does not want his people to be condemned. He wants them to turn to him. But they will not turn and change their ways if they think they are fine the way they are. A doctor who tells you everything is fine when he knows you have a malignant tumor is not helping you with good news. He is fooling you and placing you in peril by pretending all is well. God says, "Do not pray for them" out of love, not because he has condemned them with no hope. They need to understand their dire situation and humbly come back to God.

That is why later Jeremiah does pray for certain people, for those he hopes will listen to the Lord (see Jeremiah 42-44). A group of army leaders ask Jeremiah to pray for them as they decide whether they should risk staying in their land or go to Egypt where they will be safe. Jeremiah agrees, prays, and asks the Lord about their situation. The Lord clearly tells them to stay and he will bless them. Nothing but disaster awaits them in Egypt. Having asked for prayer, these army leaders then proceed to do the exact opposite of what the Lord said! They even accuse Jeremiah of lying about what God said! Sometimes, it does not pay to pray for others because they are determined not to listen to God.

But it always pays to pray if we seek to follow the will of God, because we know he wills our good. So, the longest prayer in Jeremiah follows God's instruction to him to buy a field in Judah. This seems like a very bad real estate deal. Why buy a field when the army of Babylon is about to destroy Judah? Because it is a sign of hope. A sign that God's people will one day return to their land and buy fields and houses again.

So Jeremiah prays, confessing the sins of his people and proclaiming God to be just in punishing them. God replies, promising to return his people to him and to the land:

> I will surely gather them from all the lands where I banish them in my
> furious anger and great wrath; I will bring them back to this place and let
> them live in safety. They will be my people, and I will be their God. I will
> give them singleness of heart and action, so that they will always fear me
> for their own good and the good of their children after them. I will make
> an everlasting covenant with them: I will never stop doing good to them,
> and I will inspire them to fear me, so that they will never turn away from
> me. I will rejoice in doing them good and will assuredly plant them in this
> land with all my heart and soul. (Jeremiah 32:37-41)

So should we pray for everyone? Yes. No matter how far they have gone from God, he wants them back. Murderers, child molesters, greedy bankers—none are beyond the forgiveness of God. But how do we pray for them? What do we pray for? We do not pray that God will forgive them while they fool themselves into thinking what they do is right. They must come to their senses and turn to God. They (and we) must humbly seek him. Then he will gather them back. That is how we pray.

Daniel—How Much Does It Cost to Pray?

As with other prophets, Daniel's prayer life reflects his circumstances. As a young man torn from his own and brought to serve a foreign king, Daniel has to rely on the power of God. When king Nebuchadnezzar has a troubling dream, he demands on pain of death that his wise men tell him both the dream and its meaning. With his life on the line, Daniel pleads with God to reveal this mystery. God hears. He acts. He reveals. And Daniel gives thanks:

> During the night the mystery was revealed to Daniel in a vision. Then Daniel
>> praised the God of heaven and said:
> "Praise be to the name of God for ever and ever;
>> wisdom and power are his.
> He changes times and seasons;
>> he sets up kings and deposes them.
>> He gives wisdom to the wise
>> and knowledge to the discerning.
> He reveals deep and hidden things;
>> he knows what lies in darkness,
>> and light dwells with him.
> I thank and praise you, O God of my fathers:
>> You have given me wisdom and power,
>> you have made known to me what we asked of you,
>> you have made known to us the dream of the king."
>> (Daniel 2:19-23)

What do we learn about prayer here? No one threatens our lives if we do not interpret their dreams. But, like Daniel, we are asked to trust God for wisdom in situations we cannot figure out on our own. We believe when we ask that God will give us the wisdom we so much need.

From Daniel we also learn that it sometimes costs us to pray. Another king, Darius, makes a law that no one can pray to any god but the king. "Now when Daniel learned that the decree had been published, he went home to his upstairs room where the windows opened toward Jerusalem. Three times a day he got down on his knees and prayed, giving thanks to his God, just as he had done before" (Daniel 6:10). Daniel's enemies catch him praying, then denounce him to the king who throws him in the den of lions. We know how that story ends.

Does it cost us to pray? It may cost time and effort. Some might ridicule us. No one is likely to throw us to the lions. Yet in some parts of our world, those who pray to the "wrong" God are still cruelly punished. Their experiences (and Daniel's) make whatever price we pay to pray pale by comparison.

The longest prayer in Daniel is a prayer of confession.

> I prayed to the Lord my God and confessed:
>
> "O Lord, the great and awesome God, who keeps his covenant of love with all who love him and obey his commands, we have sinned and done wrong. We have been wicked and have rebelled; we have turned away from your commands and laws. We have not listened to your servants the prophets, who spoke in your name to our kings, our princes and our fathers, and to all the people of the land." (Daniel 9:4-6)

Daniel continues his prayer in this way, admitting Israel's sin and asking for God's mercy. God hears, and sends the angel Gabriel to Daniel with a vision of hope and restoration.

From Daniel, then, we learn the value of persistence in prayer. When all seems hopeless. In exile. Facing death. When we have sinned. When we do not understand. In all these circumstances, we pray.

Jonah—How Should We Not Pray?

God calls Jonah to be a prophet to Nineveh. He refuses to go. He gets on a ship headed in the opposite direction. A storm threatens all life on the ship. In the storm, does Jonah pray? No! He tells the sailors to toss him in the sea, but it is these pagan sailors who pray to the Lord, not Jonah!

Jonah only prays when a great fish swallows him. Even then, his prayer lacks repentance. He does not rejoice in the faithfulness of God. Instead, he cries in his distress. The Lord hears and delivers him from the fish.

Jonah then goes to Nineveh, proclaims the Lord's message, and the city turns to God and is saved. That only makes Jonah angry! He hates the people of Nineveh. So Jonah prays one of the strangest prayers in the Bible.

> But Jonah was greatly displeased and became angry. He prayed to the Lord, "O Lord, is this not what I said when I was still at home? That is why I was so quick to flee to Tarshish. I knew that you are a gracious and compassionate God, slow to anger and abounding in love, a God who relents from sending calamity. Now, O Lord, take away my life, for it is better for me to die than to live."
>
> But the Lord replied, "Have you any right to be angry?" (Jonah 4:1-4)

Jonah wants to die because a loving God has forgiven Jonah's enemies. It is hard to imagine the depth of his bitterness. Yet the Lord tries to teach him a lesson about concern for others.

What do we learn from Jonah? Do not pray this way! Jonah's prayers are uniformly selfish. He does not pray for the safety of the sailors (although he is willing for them to throw him overboard). He turns to God only when in deep trouble, stuck inside a fish. He is angry in prayer, not with the faithful anger of a Job, but with childish anger because he does not get his way. Yet God hears and responds to Jonah's prayer, proving that the Lord is gracious even to those who pray badly.

Habakkuk—How Do We Pray in Disaster?

Contrast Habakkuk with Jonah. Jonah brings his trouble on himself through bad actions and attitudes. Habakkuk is a victim of disaster. Destruction, violence, wickedness, war, and famine. In extreme circumstances, Habakkuk faithfully pours out his heart to God, wondering why God does not act since he is good and powerful. The Lord answers Habakkuk, telling him that justice will come. Habakkuk must wait patiently for it.

Habakkuk responds with praise and with some of the most profound words of trust found in Scripture.

Though the fig tree does not bud

and there are no grapes on the vines,

though the olive crop fails

and the fields produce no food,

though there are no sheep in the pen

and no cattle in the stalls,

yet I will rejoice in the Lord,

I will be joyful in God my Savior.

(Habakkuk 3:17-18)

Here is a cry of hope in hopelessness. This is how to pray! We rejoice easily in good health, in prosperity, and in success. But what if the stock market falls, banks fail, our savings are wiped out, we lose our job, and there are shortages of gasoline and even food? Do we cry out to God in our distress? Yes! We shout "Why?" "How long?" But we cry to God in faith, patience, and joy. He has taken care of us in the past. He will again.

Prayer is not about getting what we want. It is not even about getting what we need. It is about keeping faith with a God we do not fully understand. It is about audaciously trusting his love particularly when it looks as though there is no reason to trust. It is about learning to rely on him alone.

Questions for Further Discussion

1. Is idolatry really a problem today? Do we pray to other "gods"? How? Do we pray to God the same way others pray to their gods?

2. Is there ever a time we should not pray for others? Is there a prayer we can pray for anyone, regardless of their circumstances?

3. Does it "cost" us anything to pray? If not, is prayer valuable? If so, what is the cost? Are we willing to bear it?

4. Is there anything positive we can learn from the way Jonah prayed?

5. Can we sincerely pray when everything goes wrong? How can we pray when it seems to do no good? When it seems God does not hear?

Try This Week

Think of the worst thing you can imagine happening to you. Why would God let that happen? This week pray that God will give you the faith to pray even when everything goes wrong.

A Book to Read

Now out-of-print, Ronald E. Clements, *In Spirit and Truth: Insights from Biblical Prayers* (Atlanta: John Knox Press, 1985) discusses several prayers of individuals in the Bible.

CHAPTER 11

WHAT CAN WE LEARN ABOUT PRAYER FROM THE OLD TESTAMENT?

I will lift up the cup of salvation and call on the name of the Lord.

PSALM 116:13

How can learning of Old Testament prayer change the way we pray today? Are these merely interesting stories of how God's people once prayed? Or is there something here that can instruct and even transform us? Has prayer changed fundamentally since ancient times?

To answer these questions and to summarize prayer in the Old Testament, we turn to a young Jewish Rabbi who was immersed in the practices of prayer. His name is Jesus. He taught his disciples to pray a prayer that reflects the experience of the Hebrew Scriptures. We call it the Lord's Prayer or the Our Father. Each phrase of the prayer expresses the prayer life of God's people.

Our Father

Prayer is almost a universal human experience. Practically everyone prays. But prayer is not a merely human experience. Prayer involves every aspect of our being, but it is more than human wishes and desires. Even some devout believers sometimes speak of prayer as only changing us. Some think it is primarily positive thinking or healthy psychology.

But the Old Testament shows that prayer is primarily about God, not about us. What distinguishes the prayers of the surrounding nations to their gods from the prayers of Israel to the Lord is that the Lord truly hears. He is a God who is not far removed from his people. He is a God who wants a close, covenant relationship with them.

So although the Old Testament rarely speaks of God as Father, it does describe him as a God who comes close to his people. He walks in the garden with Adam and Eve. He appears to Abraham with promises of great blessing. Jacob wrestles with him. Moses sees him pass by. He comes to his people at Sinai. He rules through kings. He speaks through prophets. He tenderly calls his people back to him, when they repeatedly turn to other gods.

Our God is very close to us. He wants us to pray to him personally. He is the God who listens. He hears the cry of Hannah. He restores the health of Hezekiah. He can take the anguished complaint of the psalmist. Prayer is dialogue with one who cares for us like a father cares for his beloved children.

In Heaven

God is close to us but he is also beyond us. He is the Almighty. He is in heaven. We are on earth. He is God and we are not.

Abraham, Moses, and others fall on their faces before the Lord, showing their recognition of his power. They have a close relationship with him. They come to him boldly in prayer. But they are not buddies with God. They do not presume. Familiarity with the Lord does not breed contempt, but rather reverence for him.

When the Philistines capture the Ark of the Covenant, they think they have control over Israel's God. But they soon find that he does not live in the box. He reigns from heaven. When Solomon builds a temple for the Lord, he prays and confesses that no building can contain God. He asks that God will hear from heaven and will bless all who seek him at the temple. Job cries out in pain to God. He feels so close to God that he can even question why the Lord allows such suffering. But when God appears to Job in the whirlwind, then Job knows that God is beyond our questioning. He is great. We are small. Too small to understand, but not too small to praise him.

God is Father. He is close to us. But he is also in heaven. He is greater than us. That does not mean he is distant and will not hear. Instead, it means he is powerful enough to answer our prayers. The God of heaven can do anything he wills. He can overcome all obstacles. He can heal all diseases. We pray to a God who comes near, but who is beyond our imagination.

Holy Is Your Name

The heart of prayer is worship and thanksgiving to a holy and sovereign God. By recognizing that God's name is holy, we accept the call to be holy. However, holiness is quite misunderstood in our time. No one wants to be called a "holy Joe." The word stamps one as proud and superior. We cannot hear the word holy applied to someone without thinking they are "holier than thou."

But in the Bible holiness refers to the very character of God. He is unique. There is no one like him. He is good. He only gives good gifts to his children. These two aspects of holiness—being special and doing good to others—are what we confess when we pray. This is why so many of the Psalms are full of praise. We praise God for who he is. He is the uniquely good God.

By bowing before God, we become like God. He is holy and in prayer he transforms us into his holy people. A different sort of people. A genuinely good people. The Old Testament experience of prayer shows that transformative power. Abraham is not the same after his encounter with God. Even selfish Jacob changes after he wrestles with God. Job's questions are swallowed up by his encounter with a holy God who speaks from the whirlwind. Elisha's servant can see the armies of the Lord when his eyes are opened in prayer.

In prayer we praise the holy name of God. Through that praise, God shares his holy nature with us.

Your Kingdom Come

In prayer, we call on God to be present and active in the world. We do not make God show up. He is always the ruler of the world. But we become aware of his power and sovereignty in prayer.

For Israel, the royal psalms expressed that awareness. The Lord alone is king. Israel's anointed king merely represents the ultimate reign of God. Other passages make it clear that the Lord rules not only over Israel, but over every tribe and country.

By confessing that the Lord alone is king, we make the power of all other rulers dependant on him. In the prayers of David and other faithful Israelite kings, we hear their recognition that their power comes solely from the Lord. They do not rule according to their own talents, wisdom, or desires. They are to submit to the true and only King.

When Israel and we call upon the Lord as king, we also submit to his authority. Prayers of kingship are prayers pledging obedience. In a world filled with democracies, we need to learn how to pray to our King. Submission, obedience, and reverence do not come easily to those raised on individual rights. Bowing before the Almighty teaches our hearts and lives to submit. But our King is no heartless dictator. He is a gracious and loving sovereign who works for our good. Thus our submission is a joy.

Your Will Be Done

The laments of the Old Testament show that we must be honest about our desires, anger, fear, and doubts in prayer. What is more, in prayer we can question, struggle with, and even change God's will.

Abraham bargains with God for the fate of Sodom. Yet he does this face down before the Lord in humility. In essence, he says, "Your will be done." Hezekiah is told he will die. He turns his face to the wall and cries out to God. The Lord hears and preserves his life.

These and other Old Testament examples show that prayer is a genuine dialogue with God. But in this dialogue, God's people never forget that he is their Lord and King. This is shown most clearly in the lament psalms and in the dialogues between Job and God. Job is an honest but faithful lamenter who comes very close with charging God with wrongdoing. But he does not cross that line. What is more, he does not break relationship with God, even when it seems that God's will is turned against Job. In the end, God's will is done. Job's friends are silenced. Job is blessed.

Thus, praying "Your will be done" is not an easy acceptance of our lot in life. Instead, it is a courageous move that sticks with God particularly when we do not like his will. It is trusting when there is no reason to trust.

Give Us This Day

It is right and proper to make requests in prayer. Requests for physical needs, for safety, for healing, and for guidance should be made to the God who gives generously. The Lord's people never hesitate to ask for what they need.

Abraham's servant does not know how to fulfill his mission of finding a wife for Isaac. He prays and God provides. Hannah prays for a son and receives Samuel. Manoah asks for wisdom in raising his son, Samson. The woman from Shunem asks for the return of her son to life. The Lord raises him through Elisha.

In all these instances, God's people pray for what they most need and desire. They pray for daily bread, for the blessing needed in the moment. God hears and gives.

Prayer is more than making requests. It is all about relationship with God. But God as a loving Father wants his children to ask him for what they want. We should never be reticent to ask for anything, small or great, knowing that our God is both good and great.

Nothing is beyond his power. He only wants what is best for us. Requests recognize that we depend on God for food, for life, for all.

Forgive Us

Many of the prayers in the Old Testament are cries for pardon. God's people do not always trust him to provide. They ask for a king to provide and protect. God grants their request but later they realize they have rejected the Lord as their only king. They repent, pray, and are forgiven. David puts his trust in the number of fighting men he has. He realizes his sin, turns back to God, but still Israel suffers the consequences of his sin. God's people turn against him so thoroughly that he sends them into exile. There they cry to the Lord for forgiveness. He hears and returns them to their land through Ezra and Nehemiah.

From these stories we learn that we must humbly and penitently pray for pardon when we sin. Repentance is required, but forgiveness depends not on the quality of our repentance, but on the gracious Father. Even evil kings like Manasseh who practice idolatry and child sacrifice receive mercy from the Lord when they genuinely turn to him.

In word and deed, when we pray we say, "Lord be merciful to me, a sinner!" The Old Testament assures us God hears such prayers and completely pardons.

As We Forgive

Forgiveness is sometimes difficult to receive but almost always difficult to truly give. I have forgiven people several times for a single offense—which means I really did not forgive them the first time.

By contrast, we find Old Testament people forgiving and even praying for their enemies. Job prays for his friends who treated him badly. God hears and forgives. Moses often prays for Pharaoh and the Egyptians. God hears his prayers and stops the plague. Moses intercedes often for the Israelites when they turn from God to idols. He puts his life and his relationship with God on the line for them. They repay him by whining against his leadership. Still Moses continues to pray. God forgives Israel for the sake of Moses.

In prayer, we intercede for others. We speak to God on behalf of those in danger, want, pain, and sin. Praying for enemies is not easy. We do not pray because we like them or approve of what they are doing. But by sincerely asking God to bless them, we reflect a Father who cares for all. We have the strength to forgive when we remember that our God forgives us. And if we cannot open our hearts wide enough to forgive others, then we cannot truly receive the forgiveness God offers to us.

Deliver Us from Evil

Israel often faced flesh and blood enemies—Philistines, Arameans, Ammonites, and others. When surrounded by superior foes, they prayed to God for deliverance. The Lord fought their battles for them, sometimes with heavenly armies, sometimes through human soldiers.

Individual Israelites also faced those who meant them harm. David's trusted advisor Ahithophel betrays him, taking the part of the rebel Absalom. David prays for deliverance from the advice of Ahitophel. God hears and makes Absalom reject his good advice. David is spared from his enemy.

We may also face flesh and blood enemies who mean us harm. But our greatest enemy is the Evil One himself. In prayer, we place ourselves in the hands of the only one who can protect us from evil. Our security does not depend upon armies, resources, or our own strength. God alone delivers.

Praying with the Old Testament

Thus, when Jesus teaches his followers to pray, his instruction is not completely foreign to them or to us. It builds on the rich heritage of Old Testament prayer. Having looked at the prayers of those who trusted God in the past, we now can pray with deeper faith. In prayer we join hands with Abraham, Sarah, Moses, Hannah, and Elijah. More importantly, we pray in the name of one who learned to pray from the Old Testament. The one who continues to intercede for us.

In Jesus' name, let us pray.

Questions for Further Discussion

1. What does it mean to call God "Father"? If your relationship with your father was not good, does this change how you look at God?

2. Is God far removed from us? What does it mean to say he is "in heaven"?

3. What does the "kingdom of God" mean to you? What can we do to make that kingdom come?

4. What do we trust for our daily well-being? Do we truly trust God alone to bless?

5. Do you find it difficult to forgive yourself? To forgive others? If so, what might help you forgive?

Try This Week

Pray the Lord's Prayer each day this week.

A Book to Read

A recent look at several Old Testament prayers is Walter Brueggemann, *Great Prayers of the Old Testament* (Louisville: Westminster John Knox, 2008).

PART FOUR

PRAYING WITH JESUS IN THE GOSPELS

Chapter 12

"OUR FATHER"
Prayer as Relationship with the Holy

"Pray then in this way:
Our Father in heaven . . ."

MATTHEW 6:9

It's midnight. There's a knock on the door. You stumble out of bed to find a policeman there. Your two sons have been in an accident. Both are dead.

How do you pray?

You go with your Dad to the doctor. Dad is sixty-two and in good health, but lately he's been acting strange. The diagnosis: Alzheimer's disease.

How do you pray?

Another day begins. You get up at the same time, wash the same face, get in the same car, and go to the same job. You have a great family, a good career, a fine church. Life should be wonderful, but you feel empty inside.

How do you pray?

These are not hypothetical situations, but real ones. I know the people who've been in these circumstances. So do you. Perhaps you're going through them yourself. When hurt, shocked, and confused, we know prayer can help, but we sometimes can't bring ourselves to pray. We don't know how.

In times like these we appreciate the plea of the first disciples, "Lord, teach us to pray" (Luke 11:1). Their cry is ours. For in every trial and every joy in life we can turn to God in prayer. Jesus himself shows us the way, if we will but slow down, stand still, and hear his voice.

Pray in Secret
(Matthew 6:5-6)

In Matthew, almost all of Jesus' teaching on prayer takes place in the Sermon on the Mount. The primary point of the sermon is that Jesus' disciples must take care that their righteousness exceeds that of the scribes and Pharisees (Matthew 5:20). In Matthew 6, Jesus explains what that higher righteousness means in terms of outward acts of worship: giving alms, praying, and fasting. Jesus certainly commends these acts of righteousness or piety, but to exceed the practices of the Pharisees, one must do these acts for God, not to be praised by others.

Jesus gives two warnings on prayer. First, he warns against praying publicly to be seen by others:

> And whenever you pray, do not be like the hypocrites; for they love to stand and pray in the synagogues and at the street corners, so that they may be seen by others. Truly I tell you, they have received their reward. But whenever you pray, go into your room and shut the door and pray to your Father who is in secret; and you Father who sees in secret will reward you. (Matthew 6:5-6)

Christ calls us to a higher righteousness that is not a "showy" righteousness. As with almsgiving (Matthew 6:2-4), Jesus calls those who pray to be seen by others "hypocrites." This term is the Greek term for "actor," that is, someone who is playing a role. The implication here is that the hypocrites may not be completely insincere; they may truly believe in God and may be truly praying to him. The problem is they are not praying to him *alone*. Like actors they are aware of their audience, of those in the synagogue or streets who hear them. Indeed, it is this audience that they primarily wish to please; hence they have already received their reward. The approval or applause of those around them is the only answer their prayers will get. They may think they are praying to God, but in truth they have another audience.

By contrast Jesus says to have an audience of one. "Go to your room, shut the door, and pray to your Father in secret." The word translated "room" here is literally the "storeroom," the locked room in the house where valuables are kept. To pray in the storeroom is the exact opposite of praying on the street corner; here care is taken that no one but God will hear your prayer. If God alone is the audience for our prayers, then his applause is all we hear. More importantly, it is he who hears our prayers and he alone who can and will answer.

This command to "pray alone" is not a condemnation of all public or group prayer. Many scriptures speak of the importance of prayer in public worship and the power of praying with our brothers and sisters. The Lord's Prayer itself addresses God as *our* Father, implying that it was a group prayer. However, there is a strong warning here about public prayer. When leading prayer or praying with others in a small group, we certainly must consider the thoughts and feelings of those around us; after all, we are praying *with* them. But we must never forget that we are praying *to* God. It is God alone we address. It is God alone who answers prayer. It is God alone who gives our reward.

Don't Babble
(Matthew 6:7-8)

Having warned his disciples against praying like hypocrites, Jesus secondly warns them about praying like pagans: "And whenever you pray, do not heap up empty phrases as the Gentiles do; for they think they will be heard because of their many words. Do not be like them, for your Father knows what you need before you ask him" (Matthew 6:7-8).

Repeated prayers and persistence in prayer are not condemned here; Jesus himself commends these in other passages. Neither does he condemn the use of model or written prayers, since the Lord's Prayer immediately follows this. What he condemns is a "magical" view of prayer. To many pagans, prayers were much like magical incantations. What mattered was not the relation of the worshippers to their gods, but the repetition of the right phrases.

To Jesus, these types of prayer were complete nonsense. The phrase "heap up empty phrases" implies to babble meaninglessly. If such prayers are worthless when made to a pagan god, how much more are they an affront to the living

God! Scripture clearly says we should not attempt to manipulate God. He is the sovereign Lord of the universe. He knows all, including our every need, and no "magic formula" will compel him to do our bidding.

We need not babble to God for our God is a God of love. He is not an unfeeling Supreme Being that we must fool and manipulate to secure his bounties. Such were the pagan "gods." But the God of the Bible is a loving Father who not only knows our needs, but also promises to supply all we need.

The last phrase of this passage, "... your Father knows what you need before you ask him," raises one of the great unanswered questions of the Bible: "If God knows what we need before we ask, then why should we pray?" Some have speculated that prayer is simply for us, not for God. In other words, God would give us what we need whether we ask or not, but he knows that the very act of asking helps us spiritually.

While there is some truth in this statement (the act of prayer certainly helps one grow spiritually), this cannot be a complete explanation of the purpose and nature of prayer. Other New Testament passages clearly say prayer is a genuine communication with God and that it actually affects the mind of God himself. This is the most profound biblical teaching on prayer and it demonstrates clearly the amazing extent of God's love: in prayer we affect the mind of God.

We must not misunderstand this great teaching. God is not some tyrant who withholds his blessings until we ask. Nor is he a weak God who cannot bless until he hears the "magic words." This is the very view that Jesus opposes. He is a loving God who wants to bless, who knows what we need before we ask, yet who works in such a way that our will and our prayers somehow cooperate with his will in accomplishing his purposes for us.

So why pray? We could give many answers: "Because it works," "Because it is commanded," "Because Jesus and the apostles prayed," "Because we need to talk to our Father." Interestingly enough, the Bible really never tells us why we pray, it just assumes we will. The children of God pray to him. Even though he knows our needs, and wants to bless us, we pray. Because he knows our needs, and wants to bless us, we pray.

But how should we pray?

The Lord's Prayer
(Matthew 6:9-15; Luke 11:1-4)

In Luke 11, it is one of Jesus' disciples who asks, "Lord teach us to pray . . . ." In reply he says:

"Pray then in this way:
Our Father in heaven,
> hallowed be your name.
> Your kingdom come.
> Your will be done,
>> on earth as it is in heaven.
> Give us this day our daily bread.
> And forgive us our debts,
>> as we also have forgiven our debtors.
> And do not bring us to the time of trial,
>> but rescue us from the evil one."
>>> (Matthew 6:9-13)

This prayer is known as the "Our Father," the "Lord's Prayer," or the "Model Prayer." By whatever name, it is certainly the best known prayer among Christians and until recent years was known by practically everyone in the Western world. In light of Jesus' words about empty babbling, it is ironic that this prayer has been repeated countless times in the history of Christianity. No doubt most who pray the prayer are sincere and realize the significance of the words they speak, but many times the very familiarity of these words and the rote way in which we say them make it difficult to pray this prayer with the power Jesus intended.

So what new thing can one say about the Lord's Prayer? Dozens of books have been written on these few words. Any study of prayer in the New Testament has to start here, but since we know these words so well what more can we learn about them?

Perhaps little. And yet we must try. By looking again at the familiar phrases of this prayer, perhaps we can recover some of its power and realize anew why this model prayer has stood the test of time.

Note the address of the prayer, "Our Father in heaven." In this short phrase we have the great paradox of the nature of God. He is our Father. He is near, close to us.

He gently cares for us. He knows all our needs. At the same time he is in heaven. He is God, not human. He is the all-powerful ruler of the universe. He is holy. His ways are not our ways. We cannot understand or control him. By calling God our Father in heaven, we come to him boldly, as we would to our own father, but we also bow face down before him, unworthy to lift our eyes to his glory.

"Hallowed be thy name." We should hold this great God in reverence. Though we draw close to God in prayer, we bow before him, not only when we pray, but symbolically in our whole life. Each moment we must show respect for God.

But there is more to this phrase than mere reverence for God. The name of God is the way God reveals himself to humankind. Remember when Moses at the burning bush asked the name of God and God revealed it to him. So God has more fully revealed his name and nature to us in Christ. To pray that God will make his name holy is to pray that he will reveal himself in our world.

As such, this phrase is similar to the next one: "Your kingdom come." This is the pivotal point of the prayer. The Lord's Prayer is fundamentally a "kingdom prayer." To pray that God's kingdom will come is to recognize that the kingdom has already been inaugurated in the church, that God's reign is increasing in the present world, but the ultimate rule of God will not be realized until the end of time. We earnestly pray that God will reign, not only at the end, but today in our lives.

What does it mean for God to reign in our lives? It means we must be one with his will. So we pray, "Your will be done on earth as it is in heaven." This prayer has a cosmic significance. God's bidding is followed perfectly in heaven. We pray the day will come when it is followed perfectly on earth. But God's will also has a moral force in each Christian's life. If we want God's will to be done on earth, then it must begin with us. Our will must be shaped to his. Like the angels in heaven, we must always stand prepared to do his bidding.

The remainder of the prayer consists of three requests. The first, "Give us this day our daily bread," seems straightforward. However, in Greek this is the most problematic phrase of the prayer. The word translated "daily" occurs only here in the Greek New Testament. Scholars are not sure what it means. It may mean "daily bread." If so it is right for us to ask God for the physical needs of life. Most Western Christians take daily food for granted. We need to be reminded that the necessities of life, even our meals, are a gift of God, not a natural right or something we have earned. "Daily" implies Christians should not hoard their resources, relying on their wealth and not on God. God alone supplies our needs.

A good case can be made that the phrase should be translated, "give us our bread for tomorrow." If so, God calls us to be far-sighted. Planning for tomorrow is today's task. This doesn't mean we hoard our wealth or trust our plans instead of trusting God. It means God desires us to be prudent in our actions. But Jesus also points us to the ultimate tomorrow, to the great messianic banquet to be enjoyed by his followers in the coming kingdom. Thus we pray not just for bread to fill our physical hunger, but more importantly, for what John calls "the bread of life" (John 6:48).

Since we pray to "our Father in heaven," who is a holy God, we cannot pray without a sense of our own sin. We pray that our debts will be forgiven. Here sin is spoken of as a huge debt that we cannot repay, a theme Jesus repeats in the parable of the two debtors (Matthew 18:23-35). In this prayer, as in the parable, the enormity of the debt that God has forgiven prompts the disciple to forgive his debtors. The past perfect tense of the verb "as we have also forgiven our debtors," is significant. It means not that our forgiving others earns our forgiveness, but that forgiveness of others should be such a feature of the life of the disciple that it is an accomplished fact (see Matthew 6:14-15).

The final request of the Lord's Prayer is for God's help in overcoming evil, "And do not bring us to the time of trial, but rescue us from the evil one." In our age belief in Satan, "the evil one," seems silly and superstitious to some. But the unbelievable degree of cruelty we see in the world, and the inward knowledge of the depths of our own selfishness confirm what Jesus said: the evil one is close and powerful.

Though God is vastly more powerful than Satan, his children are warned against overconfidence when facing evil. We ask God to keep us from the time of trial. This is a better translation than "Lead us not into temptation," since God tempts no one (James 1:13). God however does discipline those whom he loves and tests our faith to produce endurance (James 1:3). Knowing our own weakness, however, we must not ask for those tests. Instead when Satan tempts or God tests our faith, it is the Father, not ourselves, that we must trust for deliverance.

In summary, the Lord's Prayer is essentially a kingdom prayer. Subjects in God's kingdom will pray this way. Our king in heaven is also our Father. We pray he will continue to reveal himself on earth so all humanity will reverence his name. We pray his rule will grow on the earth, until that day when all here do his bidding as completely as heavenly beings do now.

But our Father's rule has not completely come, so we need his power in our earthly walk. We pray for our earthly bread, anticipating the heavenly feast. We pray for forgiveness and the strength to forgive. We pray for escape from trial and power to overcome the evil one. We recognize that in Christ the kingdom and rule of God has already broken into our world. We pledge to live our lives under his rule. His kingdom is here! And we anticipate the day when he rules over all, when every knee bows before him.

In this way the Lord's Prayer is a model for all Christian prayer. We do more than simply pray these words or make similar petitions to God. All our prayers are like the Lord's Prayer because we are citizens of his kingdom. All of our prayers must have this same sense of anticipation that the kingdom of this world has become, is becoming, and will become the kingdom of our Lord and of his Christ.

Recently I was overwhelmed at the power unleashed at the praying of the Lord's Prayer. I was preaching the funeral of a devout Christian woman who gave freely to others. The most touching moment of the service was not the hymns, the readings, or my own poor attempts at eloquence. No, the most comforting and uplifting moment was when the entire congregation spoke aloud the Lord's Prayer. This Christian woman had requested this at her funeral and experiencing those words together brought those who loved her closer to each other and to God.

Let us never be hesitant to approach our Heavenly Father with these familiar words, words taught us by his Son.

Questions for Further Discussion

1. What are some situations where we are tempted to pray to be seen by others? Does this mean we should not pray for our food in restaurants? What can we do to make sure our prayers are between God and us alone?

2. Name some familiar phrases you hear often in public prayers. Are these "empty phrases"? What can we do to keep them from becoming so?

3. What are some ways you have seen the kingdom of God come in your life? What are some ways the kingdom still needs to come?

4. Is it easier to forgive yourself or others? What allows us to forgive others and ourselves?

5. What do you usually ask for in prayer? What does that say about your spiritual life?

Try This Week

This week pay attention to the phrases you habitually repeat in prayer. Either find new words or make an effort to give those phrases genuine meaning.

A Book to Read

Renowned biblical scholar N. T. Wright has written *The Lord and His Prayer* (Grand Rapids: Eerdmans, 1997), a brief and helpful look at the prayer.

Chapter 13

"LORD, BE MERCIFUL"
Prayer as Humble Submission

But the tax collector, standing far off, would not even look up to heaven,
but was beating his breast and saying, 'God, be merciful to me, a sinner!'

LUKE 18:13

Learning to pray is like learning to swim. There are two extreme approaches. You can read all about swimming, practice the strokes in front of a mirror, even read the biographies of great swimmers. When you finish all that, there's still one problem. You don't know how to swim!

On the other hand, someone can just throw you in the deep end of the pool. Sink or swim. There's great motivation there, but also a clear danger of drowning.

So also with prayer. We can learn all about prayer and still not pray. We learn to pray by praying. On the other hand, we need coaching to learn to pray as we should.

Jesus is our coach. The Lord's Prayer is a model for us, but it does not exhaust Jesus' teaching on prayer. In Matthew, even before Jesus speaks of secret prayer and gives the Lord's Prayer, he instructs his disciples to pray the most difficult prayer of all: prayer for one's enemies.

Prayer for Enemies
(Matthew 5:43-48)

You have heard that it was said, "You shall love your neighbor and hate your enemy." But I say to you, Love your enemies and pray for those who persecute you, so you may be children of your Father in heaven; for he makes his sun rise on the evil and on the good, and sends rain on the righteous and on the unrighteous. For if you love those who love you, what reward do you have? Do not even the tax collectors do the same? And if you greet only your brothers and sisters, what more are you doing than others? Do not even the Gentiles do the same? Be perfect, therefore, as your heavenly Father is perfect. (Matthew 5:43-48)

This too is part of the higher righteousness that exceeds that of the scribes and Pharisees. In the Old Testament, one is to treat a foreigner in some ways better than one treats a fellow Israelite. However, most of the scribes and Pharisees had re-interpreted that teaching to allow hatred for the enemy. Jesus calls his disciples back to the nature of God himself: he cares for the righteous and unrighteous, so we too must learn to love even our enemies.

But surely good Christians have no enemies! So we may think, until reality kicks us in the teeth. Don't you know people at work who smirk and roll their eyes every time you mention God or the church? Have you ever been hassled for no reason by some petty bureaucrat? Have friends ever deceived you? Do they spread lies behind your back?

For several years I taught Junior High in a Christian school. On one occasion my wife Deb asked Eric, one of my seventh graders, what he thought of me and my class (it so happened that I had gotten on to Eric pretty severely the day before). "I wish he'd die," he said. Somewhat taken aback, Deb reminded him that was not a very Christian attitude. "Okay," said Eric, "I just wish he'd fall off a mountain and break his leg." Sometimes, through no fault of our own, we make enemies. We shouldn't be surprised. Jesus had them too. They did more than wish he'd die, they killed him.

So what can it mean to love the enemy? Surely we cannot have warm feelings toward those who are doing everything in their power to destroy us. Jesus explains what this love means, and what prayer means, by adding, "Pray for those who persecute you." We cannot feel good about someone who is inflicting pain on us unjustly. But we can will his good, that is, we can desire that God will bless, not curse, such a person. Such blessing does not mean God accepts them as they are; we should pray for their repentance. Neither does love for the enemy necessarily turn them into a friend. We might pray for our persecutors and find they persecute us more severely. No matter. We still are to pray for them, because such prayer reflects the nature of the God who loved us while we were enemies (Romans 5:10).

But how can such a prayer be sincere? How can we have a heartfelt concern for the well being of one who cheats us, calls us names, harasses us, jails us, yes, who even wants to kill us? We can't. But prayer is effective even when we don't "feel like" praying. It is natural to want revenge against our enemies. But the command of Jesus and the nature of our Father run counter to our feelings. They say, "In spite of your righteous indignation, pray for the good of your persecutor." Though our feelings say otherwise, this prayer can and must be sincere. For the God who loathes our sins, still loves us. And Jesus himself prayed, "Father forgive them . . . ."

The Power of Prayer
(Mark 9:28-29; 11:20-24)

We turn now to two passages in Mark where Jesus discusses the power of prayer. In Mark 9, a father has a son with an evil spirit. He brings his son to the disciples, but they cannot cast out the spirit. Their inability leads the father to doubt Jesus, "If you are able to do anything, have pity on us and help us," he says. Jesus replies, "If you are able!-All things can be done for the one who believes." Immediately the father of the boy cries out, "I believe; help my unbelief!" (Mark 9:23-24).

Jesus then casts out the demon. His lesson on prayer is found in his reply to the disciple's question: "When he had entered the house, his disciples asked him privately, 'Why could we not cast it out?' He said to them, 'This kind can come out only through prayer'" (Mark 9:28-29). This is a strange reply. By saying "*this kind* can only come out through prayer," is he suggesting that some demons can be cast out without the power of God? I don't think so. He implies that the disciples' had too much confidence in their own power and not enough in the power of God.

There is an important lesson here for contemporary Christians. Too many times we live our lives like those around us, relying on our own abilities—common sense, psychology, self-help, technology, prosperity—to solve our problems. Like these disciples, we may not pray at all, or if we do, we turn to God in prayer as a last resort, when "this kind" of problem (one we can't solve on our own) arises. This lack of faith is not what Jesus is recommending. True faith calls for us to rely on God through prayer at all times.

The power of prayer is even more forcefully illustrated in Mark 11. Here also Jesus' teaching on prayer is in the context of a miracle. The day before, he had cursed a barren fig tree (Mark 11:12-14). The next morning, the tree is withered to its roots. This startles the disciples:

> Then Peter remembered and said to him, "Rabbi, look! The fig tree that you cursed has withered." Jesus answered them, "Have faith in God. Truly I tell you, if you say to this mountain, 'Be taken up and thrown into the sea,' and believe that what you say will come to pass, it will be done for you. So I tell you, whatever you ask for in prayer, believe that you have received it, and it will be yours." (Mark 11:21-24)

Faith that can move mountains has become a cliché among Christians. However, it is a phrase that can be misunderstood. Too many Christians have prayed for mountains in their lives to be moved and they were not. When that happens, we tend to blame it on our own lack of faith. "If only I could believe enough, then God would answer my prayers." This is not what Jesus teaches. This kind of attitude places the power in our faith or in our prayers, not in God.

Jesus warned against lack of faith when one prays. "Do not doubt in your heart," he says. But this must be understood in the context of all the biblical teaching on prayer. If God does not do what we ask in prayer, it may indeed be because of our lack of faith. Or it may be that we have asked for the wrong thing. Or it may be that it is not God's will to give it to us. Prayer is not a magical formula: ask + faith = mountains moved. Prayer is talking with God, and we must always pray with his nature and will in mind.

Having said this, it is clear that the main point of this passage is to urge us to have bold faith when we pray. Jesus' language here is exaggerated for effect (much like his "camel through the eye of a needle" language). I don't believe he wants us to move literal mountains, but he does want us to have faith in a God who can do what seems impossible. The mountains of depression, hopelessness, poverty, addiction, and pain may weigh on us more than all the Rockies combined. Yet God can move those mountains. Jesus does not want us to pray only when we are at the end of our rope, but neither does he want us to stop praying even if the rope breaks. Nothing is too great for God. In prayer, we must never doubt his power or his goodness. No situation is too bleak for prayer.

God answers the prayer of faith, but sometimes that answer can only be seen through the eyes of faith. If we pray according to God's will, then we believe that even in those times when we cannot see the mountains of difficulty move, God has still given us his blessing.

Persistence in Prayer
(Luke 11:5-13; 18:1-8)

God loves us, he wants to bless us, he knows what we need before we ask, yet he wants us to ask. Not ask just once, but to keep on asking:

And he said to them, "Suppose one of you has a friend, and you go to him at midnight and say to him, 'Friend, lend me three loaves of bread; for a friend of mine has arrived, and I have nothing to set before him.' And he answers from within, 'Do not bother me; the door has already been locked, and my children are with me in bed; I cannot get up and give you anything.' I tell you, even though he will not get up and give him anything because he is his friend, at least because of his persistence he will get up and give him whatever he needs."

"So I say to you, Ask, and it will be given you; search, and you will find; knock, and the door will be opened for you. For everyone who asks receives, and everyone who searches finds, and for everyone who knocks, the door will be opened. Is there anyone among you who, if your child asks for a fish, will give a snake instead of a fish? Or if the child asks for an egg, will give a scorpion? If you then, who are evil, know how to give good gifts to your children, how much more will the heavenly Father give the Holy Spirit to those who ask him!" (Luke 11: 5-13)

In this parable, Jesus compares God to a friend disturbed in bed at midnight. One should not press the comparison too far. The friend will not give out of friendship, but will give to get rid of the disturbing visitor. God is not like the sleepy, bothered friend. He wants to give us good things. We give our children good gifts, even though we are evil people. How much more will the good God give good gifts to us!

So the parable does not picture God as irritated or bothered by our prayers. The point of the parable is persistence. If being persistent pays off when dealing with ill, sleepy, evil men, then how much more will it pay off when we ask of our loving Father. God does not need to be told constantly of our needs to answer us. He knows them already. But we are told to be persistent, perhaps for our own sake, to mold our will to his.

There is clearly a difference between persistence in prayer and the "empty babbling" Jesus warned of earlier. Jesus is not saying that fifty prayers are better than forty, as if God counts rather than listens to prayer. What he says is "don't stop praying," as is made clear in the next parable:

> Then Jesus told them a parable about their need to pray always and not to lose heart. He said, "In a certain city there was a judge who neither feared God nor had respect for people. In that city there was a widow who kept coming to him and saying, 'Grant me justice against my opponent.' For a while he refused; but later he said to himself, 'Though I have no fear of God and no respect for anyone, yet because this widow keeps bothering me, I will grant her justice, so that she may not wear me out by continually coming.'" And the Lord said, "Listen to what the unjust judge says. And will not God grant justice to his chosen ones who cry to him day and night? I tell you, he will quickly grant justice to them. And yet, when the Son of Man comes, will he find faith on the earth?" (Luke 18:1-8)

Here again Jesus makes a comparison that seems unflattering to God. God is compared to an evil judge who cares nothing for others, but who will grant justice to a widow simply so she will leave him alone. Again, we have here a lesser to greater comparison. If someone as rotten as this judge will vindicate the widow just because of her persistence, then how much more readily will the God of love grant justice to his chosen ones?

In Luke's day this parable would be good news indeed. Many in the early church had undergone ridicule, imprisonment, and torture for their faith. They had cried to God for justice, for vindication, but he had not yet rescued them. They were losing heart.

For us who live nineteen hundred years later, the parable is still welcome news. At times it seems that evil is triumphant in the world. As Christians our lives are quite strange to those around us. They cannot understand why we do not live for the moment as they do. We forgo temporary pleasures—wealth, hedonism, power— because we believe a new world is coming. Yet it appears that new age has been delayed, Christ has not yet returned, so we are tempted to lose heart. Those around us appear to have more fun, more life, indeed, even more sense than we do. They look like realists and we look like dreamers, wishing for a world that does not exist. But we know better. We know the true reality. Yet we long to be vindicated. We want those around us to see that we were right all along. We want every knee to bow before the Lord Jesus.

And so we pray and do not lose heart, for God will speedily vindicate us. We pray in light of that reality that unbelievers cannot see. We pray knowing the Son of Man comes quickly to grant justice. The question is: will he find us faithful?

Humility in Prayer
(Luke 18:9-14)

If our answer to the above question is, "Of course he will find us faithful," if we feel our salvation is assured because of our righteousness or perhaps even because of our "spiritual" prayers, Jesus warns us in a third parable against spiritual pride in prayer:

He also told this parable to some who trusted in themselves that they were righteous and regarded others with contempt: "Two men went up to the temple to pray, one a Pharisee and the other a tax collector. The Pharisee standing by himself, was praying thus, 'God, I thank you that I am not like other people: thieves, rogues, adulterers, or even like this tax collector. I fast twice a week; I give a tenth of all my income.' But the tax collector, standing far off, would not even look up to heaven, but was beating his breast and saying, 'God, be merciful to me, a sinner!' I tell you, this man went down to his home justified rather than the other; for all who exalt themselves will be humbled, but all who humble themselves will be exalted." (Luke 18:9-14)

Contemporary audiences are apt to hear this parable in a way completely opposite from how it was heard originally. To us the Pharisee is the bad guy from the beginning. When we hear Pharisee, we immediately think hypocrite. We don't expect his prayer to be answered. By contrast, we know that the tax collectors were companions to Jesus, so they can't be all bad.

Jesus' listeners would have known better. After all, the Pharisees were those who took God's word seriously. Their whole lives were spent in devotion to him. They kept the law in every detail. They gave to the poor. They fasted. Their motto was, "God said it; I believe it; that settles it." And they certainly knew how to pray.

Tax collectors were traitors. They took the hard-earned money from God's people and gave it to a pagan government. They cared not for God or his law, but lived only to line their own pockets. For a tax collector to pray would be a waste of time.

So this parable must have shocked those who first heard it, though it fails to shock us. It was unthinkable that a Pharisee's prayer would not be heard, but a tax collector's would. But that is precisely what happened. "All who exalt themselves will be humbled, but all who humble themselves will be exalted."

Contemporary Christians cannot hear this parable unless we identify with the Pharisee. Like him, we love God; we want to keep his law; we pray to him regularly. Like the Pharisee, we too are appalled by those who despise God's laws—child molesters, murderers, thieves, corrupt politicians—and we thank God we are not like them. We might even read this parable and thank God that we are not hypocritical like this Pharisee.

Jesus speaks this parable to us. Prayer must never be a time to rejoice in our own righteousness. Only one is righteous. It is the one to whom we pray. We come to this holy God in the filthy rags of our own righteousness. Yes, we are to approach him boldly. Yes, he is our loving Father. But we still always come with these words, "Lord, be merciful to me, a sinner!"

Questions for Further Discussion _____

1. Do you have enemies? If people don't like you, is it your fault or is it because you try to follow God? What are some ways we show love for enemies?

2. What are some examples you have seen of the power of prayer? How about recent examples you have heard or read about that power?

3. Why should we be persistent in prayer if God knows what we need before we ask? Do we nag God into blessing us?

4. Do you ever compare yourself to those in the world? To other Christians? Should we? How do such comparisons affect our prayers?

5. Have you ever kept a prayer journal to remind you how God answers prayer? Did it help?

Try This Week

Practice persistence in prayer by praying about one specific situation each day this week. At the end of the week reflect on that experience.

A Book to Read

A marvelous collection of wisdom on praying is *The Contemporaries Meet the Classics on Prayer* (West Monroe, La.: Howard Publishing, 2003), compiled by Leonard Allen.

Chapter 14

"Father, I Thank You"
Prayer as the Practice of Jesus

"Father, I thank you for having heard me. I knew that you
always hear me, but I have said this for the sake of the crowd
standing here, so that they may believe that you sent me."

John 11:41-42

While we take Jesus' teaching on prayer seriously (after all, he is our Lord), we may tend to overlook the significance of Jesus' own prayers. We may conclude that his prayers are too "spiritual" to be an example for us. But that cannot be the case, for Jesus came to show us how to live in communion with the Father. We may think he never had to struggle to find an answer to prayer, since he had a "direct pipeline" to God. The prayers in Gethsemane prove otherwise. Jesus' prayers are human prayers, the prayers of one who faithfully wrestles with the will of God. We may sometimes simply read past the prayers of Jesus in the Gospels because they occur in stories of his teaching and miracles. In a hurry to get to the point of the story, we ignore the prayers along the way. But we cannot understand the life of Jesus or be his disciples without understanding his prayer life.

Blessing Food
(Matthew 14:19; 15:23; 26:26; Luke 24:30)

In the Gospels, whenever Jesus distributes food, he first blesses it. At the feeding of the five thousand (Matthew 14:19) he "blessed and broke the loaves," and at the feeding of the four thousand (Matthew 15:36) "after giving thanks he broke them...." At the Last Supper, he "took a loaf of bread and after blessing it he broke it, gave it to the disciples, and said, 'Take, eat; this is my body.'" Even the resurrected Jesus, when eating with the two men on the way to Emmaus, "took bread, blessed and broke it, and gave to them" (Luke 24:30).

It is easy to overlook the blessing of the food in these stories, because the stories themselves are so grand. In the first two stories, Jesus performs astounding miracles: he feeds five thousand and then four thousand people with a handful of food, but in each case he takes time to say the blessing. The Last Supper is touching because it is the last time Jesus is with the disciples before his death. Still he says the blessing. More significantly, he begins a ritual repeated countless times in many places throughout the centuries, a ceremony known by many names including the Eucharist, the "giving of thanks." In the Emmaus story, the blessing of the bread is so characteristic of Jesus that it opens the disciples' eyes to his true identity.

But what does it mean to "bless the bread"? In some passages another term is used: to give thanks. When Jesus blessed bread, he gave thanks to the Father who provides. He not only teaches his disciples to pray for daily bread, but by his example teaches us to be grateful for it. Blessing the bread gives thanks to God and calls on him to bless it for his service. Our food comes from God and is also for God; we eat to live for him.

Prayer for food was once a habit among Christians. Every time we ate we "asked the blessing." Among many Christians this custom is fading away. Perhaps it is because we eat on the run so often today; seldom do we have a sit-down meal with our families. But wasn't Jesus as busy, as "on the run," as we? Yet he took time to pray.

Perhaps we neglect prayer for food because it seems so trivial, so rote. We pray the same prayer every time. After all, the first prayer most of us learned was, "God is great, God is good, let us thank him for our food." Such a prayer may seem childish to us now, so childish that we stop praying at meals altogether. But wasn't prayer for food a habitual practice of Jesus? Did he not mean it every time?

146

Or perhaps we do not pray for food because we take it for granted. We've never been really hungry. Our refrigerators, pantries, and supermarkets are stocked. We may have been through some hard times, but we've never had to beg for food. Yet Jesus, who had the power to turn stones to bread, still trusted the Father to provide, and he gave thanks for all he received. Let's restore the habit of thanking God and asking his blessing on each meal we enjoy.

Private Prayer
(Matthew 14:22-23; Mark 1:35; Luke 5:16)

Jesus' habit of prayer was not confined to public prayers for food; he also had a habit of private prayer with God. After his public display of power in feeding five thousand, he needed to get away from the crowd to be alone with his Father. "Immediately he made the disciples get into the boat and go on ahead to the other side, while he dismissed the crowds. And after he had dismissed the crowds, he went up the mountain by himself to pray" (Matthew 14:22-23). Jesus practiced what he preached. He prayed not to be seen by others, but spoke to his Father secretly.

Another time, after a long day of healing, Jesus rose early to be by himself to pray. "In the morning, while it was still very dark, he got up and went out to a deserted place, and there he prayed" (Mark 1:35). Jesus' popularity as a healer and teacher forced him to make a special effort to get away for prayer. "But now more than ever the word about Jesus spread abroad; many crowds would gather to hear him and to be cured of their diseases. But he would withdraw to deserted places and pray" (Luke 5:15-16).

Withdrawing to pray alone was a constant feature of Jesus' life. To him prayer was not just a religious ceremony to be done in the synagogue, not just a custom before meals, and not just a last resort in times of trial. Prayer was the lifeblood of Jesus. Whether late at night or early in the morning, Jesus had to make time to be alone with his Father.

Christians today hear and talk quite a bit about "quiet time." We recognize the value of setting aside a time when we can be alone to pray to God and reflect on his word without being disturbed. But few of us do it on a regular basis. We live in such a busy world where our jobs, our families, and the pressures of life do not leave us the luxury of not being disturbed.

But no matter how busy we are, we cannot be busier than Jesus. Who among us is as popular as Jesus? Who has more demands on his time? Do we travel as much? Do we constantly have to deal with crowds? Do we have no refuge, no "place to lay our head"?

Perhaps Jesus had a secret that we fail to grasp. We feel the need and even think it our right to go on vacation to get away from it all. Jesus never took a vacation. But he did make the effort to get away. He made time to pray. Oh, there's nothing wrong with a vacation, but we might be missing the rejuvenating power that Jesus tapped into. If God is truly our Father, then we, like Jesus, must take time alone to talk with him. If we don't, we've missed the point of prayer and the essence of what being God's child is all about. We fail to find that true rest and relaxation that comes from being on the mountain with God.

Prayer at the Turning Points of Life

Jesus had a habit of quiet times with the Father, but as a human being he also knew times when prayer was a cry for help and guidance. In the crises of life, in those times of trial that determine what a person is made of, Jesus prayed. It is not just coincidence that precisely in these times of prayer and crisis, Jesus is most fully revealed as the Son of God. It is also true that it is precisely in such times that our own discipleship is tested and demonstrated.

Baptism (Luke 3:21-22)

The baptism of Jesus marked his entry into public life. It revealed him as "the one who is coming," the one for whom John the Baptist prepared the way. In baptism we see Jesus as a man, identifying with our sinful need for repentance. In baptism we see him as the beloved Son of God, pleasing to the Father.

All Christians are familiar with the story of Jesus' baptism. "The heaven was opened, and the Holy Spirit descended upon him in bodily form like a dove. And a voice came from heaven, 'You are my Son, the Beloved, with you I am well pleased'" (Luke 3:21-22). What we may have forgotten about this familiar story is Luke's revelation that this all happened as Jesus was praying (Luke 3:21).

Prayer and baptism. It seems at first an odd combination. On further reflection, how appropriate it is for Jesus to pray as he begins his public ministry. How appropriate for God to answer his prayer with the Spirit (did not Jesus later say the Father would grant the Holy Spirit to those who asked?). How appropriate for the Father to answer Jesus' prayer with a proclamation of his pleasure in the actions of his beloved Son.

Prayer and baptism. Not an odd combination for Jesus. Not an odd combination for his disciples. After all, isn't baptism a prayer, "an appeal to God for a good conscience, through the resurrection of Jesus Christ" (1 Peter 3:21)? In baptism we pray for the greatest gift of all: our salvation. We pray that God by grace through the death of Jesus will look upon us as his beloved children, and will pronounce himself "well pleased" with us. In baptism, Jesus was pledging his will as one with the Father. He was beginning his public ministry with prayer for the help of the Spirit. In baptism, we too make a pledge of loyalty to God and receive the gift of the Spirit (Acts 2:38). Our baptism, like Jesus', was a prayer.

Choosing the Twelve (Luke 6:12-16)

All Christians yearn to know God's will in times of decision. Does God want me to marry this person? Does he want me to take this job? To buy that house? To attend that church? The choice is made more difficult when other people are involved. When we must decide who should be promoted at work, who should lead our country, and who should lead our church, we need special wisdom and guidance.

Jesus too needed help from the Father at decision time. One of the most important decisions he made concerned those who would lead his flock after he departed. Whom should he choose to be apostles? No doubt, our choices would have been different. The ones he chose were something of a motley crowd: zealots, tax collectors, and fishermen. They were uneducated, rough, impulsive men. From a human point of view, none seemed suited for leadership.

But we know the rest of the story. We know that through the power of God and the gift of the Spirit, these apostles became champions of the faith and loving shepherds of the flock. They gave their lives to Jesus, their Lord and Master.

So how did Jesus make such a good decision? Did his insight into people make it easy? Was he just lucky? No. He made this decision through prayer: "Now during those days, he went out to the mountain to pray; and he spent the night in prayer to God. And when day came, he called his disciples and chose twelve of them, whom he also named apostles" (Luke 6:12-13).

If Jesus felt the need to spend all night in prayer to the Father before he made this momentous choice, don't we need to trust the Father with our decisions? Too many times we make crucial decisions based only on earthly wisdom, on what seems best when we weigh our options. Or worse, we make choices based on an irrational inward feeling, on how things strike us at the moment. Jesus shows us another way: pray about the decision and God will answer you. That answer may be consistent with conventional wisdom and ones deepest feelings or it may go counter to both. There is no simple formula for knowing how God helps in decision making. But Jesus believed in praying through the great decisions of life. So should we.

Revealing Himself as Messiah (Luke 9:19-22)

"Who is Jesus?" is the most important question in history. The way we answer that question determines our destiny. In Jesus' own ministry, he revealed his identity gradually. Even the twelve he chose after prayer came to know Jesus' full identity only after a slow process. The first full confession of the nature of Jesus came in response to a question he posed to the apostles during prayer:

> Once when Jesus was praying alone, with only his disciples near him, he asked them, "Who do the crowds say that I am?" They answered, "John the Baptist; but others, Elijah; and still others, that one of the ancient prophets has arisen." He said to them, "But who do you say that I am?" Peter answered, "The Messiah of God." (Luke 9:18-20)

This great confession of Peter is the foundation for the church (Matthew 16:17-18) and the foundation of our lives as Christians. To be a Christian is to confess Jesus as the Messiah of God. Note that this greatest of questions ("Who do you say that I am?") and the greatest of answers ("The Messiah of God") takes place when Jesus is praying. Through prayer he reveals himself to the disciples. In prayer we today also see Jesus as he truly is. When we pray, we join him in prayer, and we come to a deeper understanding of his nature as our Savior from God.

The Transfiguration (Luke 9:29-36)

Soon after his confession of Jesus as Messiah, Peter (along with James and John) is allowed to see the Christ in all his glory:

> Now about eight days after these sayings Jesus took with him Peter and John
> and James, and went up on the mountain to pray. And while he was pray-
> ing, the appearance of his faced changed, and his clothes became dazzling
> white. Suddenly they saw two men, Moses and Elijah talking to him. They
> appeared in glory and were speaking of his departure, which he was about
> to accomplish in Jerusalem. (Luke 9:28-31)

Peter is again the spokesman, calling for memorial dwellings to be built for Jesus, Moses, and Elijah. No doubt Peter meant this to be a compliment to Jesus, placing him on a par with the great lawgiver and the great prophet. But Luke says Peter didn't know what he was saying (Luke 9:33). Instead, just as at Jesus' baptism, a voice speaks from a cloud saying, "This is my Son, my Chosen; listen to him!" (Luke 9:35).

On the two great occasions where God confesses from heaven that Jesus is his Son, Jesus is praying. It is while Jesus is in prayer that God calls him the Beloved. It is in prayer that he receives the Spirit. It is in prayer that he is glorified. Luke is tell-ing us that believers have the same avenue to God. In prayer we not only see Jesus, but God recognizes us as he recognized his Son. While praying, we too are marked as children of God. Our clothes may not glisten and we may not meet any prophets, but we too are transfigured in prayer, transfigured into the shape of the Beloved Son.

The Raising of Lazarus (John 11:41-44)

The theme of Jesus being revealed in prayer is carried forward by one of the most amazing miracle stories in the Gospels: the raising of Lazarus from the dead. Jesus hears Lazarus is ill, but waits two days until he knows he is dead. He then takes his dis-ciples to Bethany where he meets Mary and Martha, the dead man's sisters. He orders the stone removed from the tomb, even though Lazarus had been dead four days.

> So they took away the stone. And Jesus looked upward and said, "Father,
> I thank you for having heard me. I knew that you always hear me, but I
> have said this for the sake of the crowd standing here, so that they may
> believe that you sent me." When he had said this, he cried with a loud voice,
> "Lazarus, come out!" The dead man came out, his hands and feet bound with
> strips of cloth, and his face wrapped in a cloth. Jesus said to them, "Unbind
> him, and let him go."(John 11:41-44)

In this passage we may overlook the prayer because of the greatness of the miracle. And what a miracle! A man dead four days is brought immediately back to life. But the miracle takes place only through prayer. It looks at first as if Jesus is ignoring his own teaching about praying to be seen by others. After all, doesn't he say he is praying only "for the sake of the crowd standing here"? But no. He is not praying for publicity. What we have here is a public prayer that reflects a previous private prayer, a testimony that gives the glory to God.

Note closely what Jesus says: "I thank you for having heard me." Jesus had already prayed secretly, asking the Father to raise Lazarus. He knew his Father had already answered that prayer. But he prays publicly, not so others might think him pious, but so they might know that the power of the miracle came from God: "So they may believe that you sent me." Again Jesus is revealed in prayer as one sent by the Father.

This passage serves as a commentary on Jesus' own teaching on the power of prayer. No one, not the disciples, not the crowd, and certainly neither Mary nor Martha, expected Lazarus to be raised. Even when Jesus plainly tells Martha, "Your brother will rise again," she misunderstands and thinks he is talking of the resurrection at the last day. No one can be raised from the dead. It is impossible. But Jesus did the impossible through a daring prayer.

How many times do we fail to pray for the impossible? I have a boyhood friend. At one point we were closer than brothers, but our lives took different paths. I remember as a fifteen-year-old having long conversations with "Bob" (not his real name) about our mutual faith in Jesus and our excitement in studying the Bible (okay, I'll admit we were strange teenagers). But in later years he began to drink, alienated his family and friends, and became a complete recluse. I tried more than once to talk to him about his relationship to the Lord, but he rebuffed me with laughter or with anger. Eventually (I confess) I gave up on Bob and even forgot about him in my prayers. He seemed beyond hope of change. Impossible.

But others continued to pray for Bob and an amazing thing happened. Like the demon-possessed man of old, he was "in his right mind" the next time I saw him, having returned to the Lord and to the church.

Is there a Bob in your life? One who is as spiritually dead as Lazarus was physically dead? Don't stop praying for them. The God who raised Lazarus by the power of Jesus' prayer can do what cannot be done.

Jesus as a Man of Prayer

Jesus was a man of prayer. He prayed in the ordinary course of life. He prayed for what we sometimes take for granted, for daily food. He made time to be alone with God. But he also prayed during the crises of life, those times when his faith was sorely tested. At his baptism, he was praying to his Father and he was answered from the cloud. Before he chose the twelve he prayed. Before he asked them to confess him, he prayed. He was praying when revealed in glory on the mountain. He prayed for power to raise the dead.

In all this Jesus is our example. We too bless our food. We too make time for secret prayer. We also pray in faith to the God who can raise the dead and do other impossible things. But we believe when we pray we are not only following Christ's example, we are also praying with him and he with us. We pray in his name. And like him we know our Father always hears us.

Questions for Further Discussion

1. Do you always pray before meals? Is this a good habit to cultivate? Can it become an empty habit? What might prevent that?

2. Do you have a time set aside for private prayer each day? If so, when? If not, what keeps you from this habit of prayer?

3. Is baptism a prayer? If so, how does it relate to the "sinner's prayer" that many urge those outside of Christ to pray?

4. In what sense do we see Christ revealed and transfigured in prayer? Do we better understand who he is when we pray?

5.   Since Jesus prayed out loud at the tomb of Lazarus, is there a place for Christians to pray to be seen by others? Does this contradict Jesus' teaching to pray in secret?

Try This Week

If you have not set aside a time for daily prayer, do so this week. If you already have such a time, then try a new way of praying each day this week.

A Book to Read

Eugene Peterson's *Praying with Jesus: A Year of Daily Prayers and Reflections on the Words and Actions of Jesus* (New York: HarperCollins, 1993) is an insightful daily guide that focuses on the prayer life of Jesus.

Chapter 15

"Not My Will but Yours"
Prayer as Crucifixion

"My Father, if this cannot pass unless I drink it, your will be done."

MATTHEW 26:42

Jesus had a habit of private prayer. Wouldn't it be great to listen in on one of those prayers? How exciting, how helpful it would be to hear how he spoke to the Father.

Jesus prayed in the crises of life. Wouldn't it be a comfort at times of confusion and decision in our lives to hear Jesus' words as he prayed in pain?

Intercessory Prayer (John 17)

We can hear his words. One chapter in the New Testament, John 17, is an extended prayer of Jesus. This long prayer is, no doubt, typical of the way Jesus prayed secretly to the Father, but it also is a prayer of crisis, his prayer after the Last Supper just before he is betrayed. Having dismissed Judas the betrayer from the Supper, he plainly tells his disciples, "I am with you only a little longer" (John 13:33). In John, this prayer is Jesus' final prayer before the crucifixion, yet with the cross before him, he prays less for himself than for his disciples.

In the first part of the prayer, Jesus recognizes his work will soon be complete:

After Jesus had spoken these words, he looked up to heaven and said, "Father, the hour has come; glorify your Son so that the Son may glorify you, since you have given him authority over all people, to give eternal life to all whom you have given him. And this is eternal life, that they may know you, the only true God, and Jesus Christ whom you have sent. I glorified you on earth by finishing the work that you gave me to do. So now, Father, glorify me in your presence with the glory I had in your presence before the world existed." (John 17:1-5)

Jesus is so dedicated to going to the cross that he speaks as if the deed is already done: "I glorified you on earth by finishing the work that you gave me to do." He also displays his trust in God's faithfulness: since Jesus has completed his task, God will glorify him. This is an obvious reference to the resurrection. Although Jesus heads to the cross, he prays in faith that God's power will accomplish the impossible, that through this horrible death he will be brought to life and glory. As Christians take up the cross daily, we too in prayer trust the faithful God who brings triumph and glory out of death and defeat.

Even facing death, Jesus' thinks not of himself but of his disciples. The bulk of this prayer is for "those whom you gave me" (John 17:9). He had already promised these disciples that he would not leave them "orphaned," but would give them the Holy Spirit to teach and guide them (John 14:18-26). Still, he is concerned for the safety of the disciples, because he knows persecution awaits them:

I have given them your word, and the world hated them because they do not belong to the world, just as I do not belong to the world. I am not asking you to take them out of the world, but I ask you to protect them from the evil one. They do not belong to the world, just as I do not belong to the world. Sanctify them in your truth; your word is truth. As you have sent me into the world, so I have sent them into the world. And for their sakes I sanctify myself, so they also may be sanctified in truth. (John 17:14-19)

Here is the essence of discipleship: God has sent us into the world, yet we do not belong in the world. God's word, the truth, has sanctified us. It has marked us off as God's own people and the world hates us for it. But just as Christ loved the world and was sent into it, so we disciples are sent into the world for the sake of Christ.

Much is to be learned from these words of prayer. Today we Christians do not always realize the precarious position we occupy in this world. Too many of us have made peace with this world and feel quite at home in it. In contrast to these "worldly Christians," the true disciple will always face danger from the world. Jesus foresaw this danger and prayed for God to protect his followers. We also should pray to God for strength and protection from a world that so easily distracts us from the business of discipleship.

These words also teach us about intercessory prayer. Facing imminent death, Jesus thought not of himself, but of his disciples. How many of our own prayers, particularly during crises, are centered solely on our personal needs and wants? Like Jesus, we learn to pray for others, for their physical needs, for health and food. We learn to pray for their emotional needs, for peace and joy. We pray, as Jesus did, for their spiritual needs, that God will keep them safe from the evil one. And we learn to pray even for our enemies, for those still in the world, that their eyes may be opened to the love of God in Christ.

Once a boy of five at our church taught me this lesson of care for others. Walt was a typical five-year old, full of life and smart as a whip. Born with a bone weakness, he had recently broken his leg for the fifth time. In a cast and in pain, Walt was told about an older woman in our church, a friend of his, who had passed away. "She'll have a new body!" he said with glee. Though his own body had betrayed him, Walt could rejoice with others. In the same way, facing death, Jesus thought of us.

One could hear Jesus praying only for the disciples of his day. But he also prays for us:

> I ask not only on behalf of these, but also on behalf of those who will believe on me through their word, that they all may be one. As you, Father, are in me and I in you, may they also be in us, so that the world may believe that you have sent me. The glory that you have given me I have given them, so that they may be one, as we are one, I in them and you in me, that they may become completely one, so that the world may know that you have sent me and have loved them even as you have loved me. Father, I desire that those also, whom you have given me, may be with me where I am, to see my glory, which you have given me because you loved me before the foundation of the world. (John 17:20-24)

We who have believed in Christ through the apostles' word are also included in this prayer. Jesus prayed for us! Yet, in light of the current situation of the church, his prayer is a challenge: he prays that all believers may be one. Sadly, the history of the church has mainly been the history of Christian disunity. Even today, we spend much of our energy focusing on what divides rather than what unites Christians. If Jesus prayed for unity, then we cannot call him Lord and at the same time fight with our Christian brothers and sisters.

Christian unity begins with the unity of the Father and the Son. Only by being in union with them are we united with one another. And only in that union will the world know the One whom God sent (John 17:23). A wise Christian teacher once told me that the problem with most Christians is that they are too concerned with being "right." If I care only that I am right and you are wrong, we can never have unity. But if we both realize that only God himself is ultimately "right," then our focus will be on being close to him. And the closer we get to him, the closer we get to each another. This is the key to Christian unity: we are one only in Christ.

But Christ prays an even more astonishing prayer for us: he prays we will see him in his glory. Jesus had faith that God would raise him from the dead and would glorify him in heaven. This Jesus who calls us to die with him also prays for us to share in his resurrection and his glory.

Jesus concludes his prayer by speaking of love: "Righteous Father, the world does not know you, but I know you; and these know that you have sent me. I made your name known to them, and I will make it known, so that the love with which you loved me may be in them, and I in them" (John 17:25-26). In the Lord's Prayer, Jesus prays that God's name will be made holy. Here he says he has made that holy name known to his disciples: that name is love. To know God is to know love. This is the essence of Jesus' prayer for us, that we know the love of God. Jesus, the love of God incarnate, wants to be in us. We pray that God's love will fill our lives. We pray that Christ will be in us.

Gethsemane
(Matthew 26:36-46; Mark 14:32-34; Luke 22:39-46)

Yes, Jesus had faith in the Father's goodness. He trusted God to bring him through death and to glorify him. But he also knew that prayer could change the will of God.

Facing an unjust, shameful, and cruel death, Jesus prayed to be delivered; he prayed to change God's will:

> Then Jesus went with them to a place called Gethsemane; and he said to his disciples, "Sit here while I go over there and pray." He took with him Peter and the two sons of Zebedee, and began to be grieved and agitated. Then he said to them, "I am deeply grieved, even to death; remain here, and stay awake with me." And going a little farther, he threw himself on the ground and prayed, "My Father, if it is possible, let this cup pass from me; yet not what I want, but what you want." Then he came to the disciples and found them sleeping; and he said to Peter, "So, could you not stay awake with me one hour? Stay awake and pray that you may not come into the time of trial; the spirit indeed is willing, but the flesh is weak." Again he went away for the second time and prayed, "My Father, if this cannot pass unless I drink it, your will be done." Again he came and found them sleeping, for their eyes were heavy. So leaving them again, he went away and prayed for the third time, saying the same words. Then he came to the disciples and said to them, "Are you still sleeping and taking your rest? See, the hour is at hand, and the Son of Man is betrayed into the hands of sinners. Get up, let us be going. See, my betrayer is at hand." (Matthew 26:36-46)

In Gethsemane Jesus struggles with the same question that often confronts us: what is God's will for us? We know God's ultimate will is for us to be his sanctified people and live with him in glory. But what is his will for us in time of suffering? God loves us; surely he does not want us to suffer. We are his children; he gives only good gifts to us. However, the Bible makes it clear that pain and suffering can be for our own good. Yes, we are God's children, but "the Lord disciplines those whom he loves, and chastises every child which he accepts" (Hebrews 12:6). But surely not all suffering is God's will. How can we know whether it is or not? Can't God change his mind?

Jesus faced this same dilemma. He had predicted his death and resurrection (Matthew 26:2, 32). He knew on one level that it was God's will for him to die on the cross. Yet he had to wonder, "Could God change his mind?" So, grieved and agitated, he prayed.

In this time of crisis and decision, Jesus had to face the Father, but he also wanted his disciples near. He asks Peter, James, and John to share this burden of grief with him. All they could do was sleep. Many times before, Jesus had escaped from the disciples to be alone in prayer. This time he needs them to watch with him. But they would not. He was alone.

Alone—but with his Father. He prayed the first time, "If it is possible, let this cup pass from me." There was still hope that the Father had changed his mind, that he had found another way, that it was possible for Jesus to avoid the cross. But if the Father wanted him to die, Jesus was willing.

After finding the disciples asleep, Jesus prayed a second time. This prayer is slightly different: "If this cannot pass unless I drink it, your will be done." Jesus was coming to realize that there was no other way but through the cross. Through prayer, he was learning the will of the Father. He goes and finds the disciples asleep again; he prays a third time; he sees the betrayer coming. Now he is ready for the crisis, for the cross, because he had prayed for the will of his Father.

We will probably never face this same situation. It is unlikely we will be called to give our life in obedience to God's will. But many early Christians faced their own Gethsemanes. The night before they were to be burned alive, or thrown to lions, or crucified like their Lord, they must have prayed this prayer: "Please let this pass, but your will be done." God willed that many be martyred, but through his grace in Christ he gave them strength to be faithful to death, just as he strengthened Jesus in the Garden.

No, we may not be called upon to die, but in another way, we Christians today do face our own Gethsemanes. We may not struggle with a horrible death for our faith, but we do face the battle of our will and God's will. Our problem may not be knowing God's will, but doing it. Like Peter, we find our spirit willing but our flesh weak. The cup we may want to pass is not persecution, but responsibility.

We know God's will is for us to overcome temptation, to live for others, to do what is right. We know he calls us to be faithful to our spouses, to nurture our children, to care for the stranger, and to love the church. Unlike Christ, we agonize not over God's will, but over our own. But if he had the courage to go to a literal cross, then through him we can find the courage to take up the daily cross of obedience to the Father's will.

On the Cross
(Matthew 27:45-46; Luke 23:34; Luke 23:46)

Prayer and the cross—they seem to go together. It is no surprise to find Jesus talking with his Father at the great crisis of his life. The first prayer from the cross is a cry: "And about three o'clock Jesus cried with a loud voice, 'Eli, Eli, lema sabachthani?' that is, 'My God, my God, why have you forsaken me?'" (Matthew 27:46).

This is a cry of pain. The pain is so intense, the scene so memorable, that Matthew records the very words Jesus spoke in Aramaic. In the past at times of crisis the Father had appeared in a cloud to proclaim Jesus as his "beloved Son." Now on the cross there is nothing but silence from the Father. At times we have all felt abandoned by God; we all have cried in pain. Jesus felt truly abandoned by God.

This cry is a cry of love. After all, Jesus feels forsaken not because of his own sin, but for ours. It is his love for us that drives him to the cross. As Paul later says, "For our sake he made him to be sin who knew no sin, so that in him we might become the righteousness of God" (2 Corinthians 5:21). What greater love can there be than to bear the pain for others?

This cry is also a cry of hope. Hope? Yes, for Jesus here is not using his own words, but is quoting the first line of Psalm 22. Jesus knew his Bible, and we can be sure he quoted this verse with the entire psalm in mind. In Psalm 22, David cries to the Lord in pain, but (as in many of the Psalms) this cry of pain ends in a confession of faith and hope in God. Though the psalmist feels forsaken, in truth he knows the Lord ". . . did not despise or abhor the affliction of the afflicted; he did not hide his face from me, but heard me when I cried to him" (Psalm 22:24).

Jesus' cry sounds like a cry of hopelessness, but although he quotes only the first verse, he knows this psalm ends in hope. Feeling abandoned by his Father, Jesus knew that God would never truly abandon his beloved son. Ultimately God would hear his cry and deliver him. And this God did by raising him from the dead.

In deep pain on the cross, feeling forsaken by his God, Jesus could think of others, even those who crucified him: Then Jesus said, "Father, forgive them; for they do not know what they are doing" (Luke 23:34). He had said, "Pray for those who persecute you." Here Jesus practices what he preached. What greater example of forgiveness can there be? If Jesus while on the cross can pray for the very people who condemned him, spat upon him, and drove the nails home, can we fail to pray for those who wrong us? Against whom do you still hold a grudge? Who is out to get you? Who belittles, ridicules, and ignores you? What is their name?

Pray for them.

Jesus' last prayer is exactly what we would expect: a prayer of trust in the Father's will. "Then Jesus, crying with a loud voice, said, 'Father, into your hands I commend my spirit'" (Luke 23:46).

Once I stood beside the hospital bed of a Christian sister facing brain surgery. I told her we were praying for her complete recovery and hoped she'd be back in church soon. She replied, "I appreciate that," then looking me in the eye she calmly said, "but if things don't work out, I'm ready to go." Two weeks later she was dead.

I am awed and humbled by such faith, for I cannot say with my whole heart, "I'm ready to go." But my prayer, our prayer, is that we have her faith and the faith of Jesus: "Into your hands I commend my spirit." In other words, "I'm ready to go." Some day each of us will face death. May we face it this way, trusting the Father with our future.

In Jesus' Name
(Matthew 18:19-20; John 14:13-14, 15:16, 16:23-27)

So how should Christians pray? To learn to pray we look to Jesus. We follow his great teachings on prayer. We learn to pray as he prayed, to have a habit of private prayer and to trust God in prayer during the crises of life. But that is not all. We also pray in the name of Jesus (Matthew 18:19-20; John 14:13-14, 15:16, 16:23-27). "In Jesus' name" is not some magical phrase we use to end our prayers. To pray in his name means we pray with the authority of Jesus. When we pray, he prays with us. Our prayers are his and his prayers ours.

As we turn to the rest of the New Testament to look at the prayers of the early church, let us remember that these too are the prayers of Jesus. When the disciples prayed, he prayed with them. As we learn to pray from them, we also are learning to pray like him.

Questions for Further Discussion

1. How much of your prayer life is spent in interceding for others? Do you pray more for others than yourself? Should we pray more for their physical or their spiritual well being?

2. Jesus prayed for unity among his followers. Do we? Can we pray for unity without working toward it? What are some practical ways we can promote unity?

3. What does it mean to pray, "God's will be done"? When was the last time you had trouble accepting God's will?

4. Have you ever felt forsaken by God? Was Jesus cry of being forsaken a prayer? How can we pray when we feel forsaken?

5. How do we commit our spirits to God in prayer? Is this similar to Jesus on the cross?

Try This Week

What is it that you need to surrender to Jesus? This week pray that his will, not yours, be done in that area.

A Book to Read

Richard Foster looks at several types of prayer in *Prayer, Finding the Heart's True Home* (HarperCollins, 1992). Chapter Two, "Prayer of the Forsaken," is particularly moving.

PART FIVE

PRAYING WITH EARLY CHRISTIANS IN ACTS AND THE LETTERS

Chapter 16

"THEY DEVOTED THEMSELVES TO PRAYER"
Prayer in Times of Danger

"They were constantly devoting themselves to prayer."

ACTS 1:14

Acts is the story of the church. The story of the church is the story of prayer. Yet Acts of the Apostles is one of the neglected books of the New Testament. When we do study it, we generally concentrate on the conversion stories or on Paul's missionary journeys. But Acts is a much richer book, containing a wealth of insight on what it means to be a community of disciples, including examples on how to pray.

Let's mine that wealth. In order to do so, keep two facts about Acts in mind. First, the theme of Acts is being witnesses for Jesus. At the beginning of the book, Jesus appears to the apostles for the last time, saying, "You will receive power when the Holy Spirit has come upon you; and you will be my witnesses in Jerusalem, in all Judea and Samaria, and to the ends of the earth" (Acts 1:8).

This apostolic witness through the power of the Spirit is carried on in spite of fierce opposition. Not only the apostles, but other disciples "went from place to place, proclaiming the word" (Acts 8:4). No threat could stop their witness, for their courage came not from themselves but from the Father, Son, and Spirit through prayer.

The second important fact to remember about Acts is that it is the second volume in a two-volume work. Luke tells the story of Jesus in his Gospel and the story of the church in Acts. But the story is really one. Acts is like a fifth gospel, displaying Jesus' actions on earth after his ascension. It is Jesus who sends the miracles and the Spirit at Pentecost. Jesus' name is called at baptisms and at healings. Jesus did not end his work at Calvary, or at the empty tomb, or even at his ascension. Yes, he is coming again, but in a sense he never left: he lives in the world through the church.

As we watch the church pray in Acts, we watch Jesus pray as well. Luke goes to great pains to demonstrate that the church does what Jesus did. As the disciples witness to Jesus, they become one with him. His ministry becomes their ministry; his prayers, their prayers.

Constancy in Prayer
(Acts 1:14; 2:42; 6:4)

Since the church is to pray like Jesus prayed, we are not surprised to find them constantly at prayer. In Luke, Jesus has a habit of withdrawing alone for prayer. In Acts, the disciples have the same habit of prayer: "They were constantly devoting themselves to prayer, together with certain women, including Mary the mother of Jesus, as well as his brothers" (Acts 1:14).

In Acts 1, the disciples are a confused lot, still expecting Jesus to set up an earthly kingdom (Acts 1:6). At the ascension, we find them gawking toward heaven, unsure of what to do (Acts 1:10). They are a small group, about 120 persons, not much on which to build a worldwide movement. They had not yet received the power of the Spirit. But in spite of their limitations, these disciples had learned at least one thing from their Master: they needed constantly to pray.

This habit of prayer continues after Pentecost and spreads to the new disciples: "They devoted themselves to the apostles' teaching and fellowship, to the breaking of bread and prayers" (Acts 2:42). The converts at Pentecost were all Jews; they knew their prayers, but they still needed to learn to pray as Jesus prayed. Many of these converts knew little of what Jesus had taught the apostles. Imagine their excitement at hearing the Lord's Prayer for the first time. Imagine Peter, James, and John telling of the prayer, the glory, the visitors, and the voice at the Transfiguration. Imagine their shock in learning they must pray even for their enemies. These converts learned to pray from Jesus. They learned to devote themselves to prayer.

The apostles were more than teachers of prayer; they also were devoted to prayer. When a dispute arose in the church concerning the distribution of food to widows, seven men were appointed to take care of this problem so the apostles could "devote themselves to prayer and to serving the word" (Acts 6:4). Caring for the poor is certainly an act close to the heart of God, but so is prayer. The early church neglected neither.

Most modern churches have an abundance of ministries: worship ministries, youth ministries, older-adult ministries, sports ministries, ministries to the poor, the homeless, and the sick. What about a ministry of prayer? What if some in the church were designated "prayer ministers" who, like the apostles, would devote themselves to prayer. The church would be revolutionized.

What power these early Christians had! What fellowship! What was their secret? Loyalty to Jesus? Of course. The power of the Spirit? Certainly. But they also knew the secret of prayer. The early church was a praying church. That was the source of their power. If we are to recapture their faith and their witness, we will learn to be constantly in prayer.

Prayer During the Challenges of Faith

Like Christ, the early Christians prayed during times of crisis. Although constant in prayer, they realized there were times when they especially needed God's blessing and guidance.

Choosing Workers (Acts 1:23-26; 6:1-6; 13:1-3; 14:23)

The church needs guidance when selecting leaders. Today we tend to choose leaders for the church on the basis of their leadership in the wider community. If they are successful business leaders, we assume they will be good church leaders. In most churches, the congregation has a loud voice in selecting leaders. There is no politics like church politics; the process sometimes even degenerates into a democratic one: the candidate who gets the most votes wins.

But the church is not the world and church leaders are to have a different authority from worldly leaders. The early church in Acts knew the loudest voice in choosing leaders must not belong to the congregation, but to Christ. They sought his voice in prayer.

Even before Pentecost, the 120 disciples had an important decision to make: who should take Judas' place as apostle? They proposed candidates based on specific qualifications, but the final decision they left to Jesus:

So they proposed two, Joseph called Barsabbas, who was also known as Justus, and Matthias. Then they prayed and said, "Lord, you know everyone's heart. Show us which one of these two you have chosen to take the place in this ministry and apostleship from which Judas turned aside to go to his own place." And they cast lots for them, and the lot fell on Matthias; and he was added to the eleven apostles. (Acts 1:23-26)

This decision was a crucial one. The full number of the apostles had to be complete to set the stage for Pentecost. To be an apostle was an awesome responsibility; they were to be witnesses to Jesus throughout the world.

But the disciples did not make this important decision. Jesus did. Just as he had chosen the original twelve, it is Jesus who picks Matthias. The disciples were not qualified to make this choice; Jesus alone knows the heart. So they prayed and cast lots. The lot fell on Matthias. He was numbered with the Twelve.

What exactly are lots? They were probably stones of different color, shape, or marking. These stones are placed in a receptacle, probably a bag, and then the bag was shaken until a lot was "cast" out. In this case, there were two stones, a Joseph lot and a Matthias lot, in the bag. Matthias' lot was thrown.

Why don't Christians cast lots today? I'm not sure. Perhaps we associate it with chance, superstition, or magic. The Bible never makes these associations when the lot is cast in prayer. To cast lots is to leave the decision to the Lord: "The lot is cast into the lap, but the decision is the Lord's alone" (Proverbs 16:33). This may be the real reason we are reluctant to cast lots today: we trust our own judgment more than we trust the Lord's.

However, there may be a good reason for not casting lots. The choosing of Matthias is the last time this practice is mentioned in the Bible. On Pentecost, the Holy Spirit comes upon the apostles and is promised to all who repent and are baptized (Acts 2:38). In the rest of Acts, leaders are chosen not by prayer and lots, but by prayer and the Spirit. In Acts 6, the church chooses leaders "full of the Spirit," and these seven men are appointed by the apostles through prayer and the laying on of hands (Acts 6:1-6).

Later, in Antioch, during prayer and worship the Spirit chooses Barnabas and Saul for a special work. They also are sent out on their mission with prayer, fasting, and the laying on of hands (Acts 13:1-3). On their mission, Paul and Barnabas in turn appoint elders in each church "with prayer and fasting" (Acts 14:23).

We can learn from these early Christians. The church today needs strong leaders, strong servants who will give their lives in witness to Jesus. One of the most important things a church can do is to choose good leaders. We make this choice based not on earthly standards, but on the will of God. We know his will through Scripture and through prayer. If Jesus prayed all night before selecting the apostles, if the apostles prayed as they cast lots for Matthias, if the early Christians prayed when choosing and appointing leaders, then we also must pray that the decision concerning Christian leaders will be the Lord's alone.

Although these passages primarily focus on prayer in selecting leaders, two practices associated with prayer are mentioned in passing. One is fasting. Much needs to be said about fasting. The practice is found throughout both Testaments. Many books have been written on the subject. Here we note only that fasting is closely related to prayer. Fasting does much for the body and the soul, but one thing it does is clear our minds so we can concentrate on the source not only of our food, but of our life: God alone. In fasting and prayer, one comes to know the Father's will.

The other practice associated with prayer is the laying on of hands. At first, this custom seems to signify that some power inherent in the apostles is passed on to another. However, laying on of hands is always accompanied by prayer. No human has power in himself or herself to appoint someone to a position of leadership in the church. Laying on of hands, with prayer, signifies that the appointment is made not by humans, but by God alone. He chooses leaders. He appoints leaders. Their power comes not from human authority, but from God and Christ, through the Spirit.

During Persecution (Acts 4:23-31; 12:12-17; 16: 25-34; 7:59)

The Christians in Acts faced great persecution. They lived from moment to moment knowing they might be called on to suffer and even die for their witness to Jesus. The word martyr comes from the Greek word "witness." In their moments of fear and pain, it was prayer that sustained these early disciples.

The first mention of opposition comes in Acts 4 where Peter and John are arrested for healing a lame man in the name of the resurrected Jesus. The Jewish authorities order them not to preach in the name of Jesus. They reply, "We cannot keep from speaking about what we have seen and heard" (Acts 4:20). Astounded by their boldness, the authorities threaten them and release them.

After their release, Peter and John find the rest of the disciples, recount their story, and then they all pray:

And now, Lord, look at their threats, and grant to your servants to speak your word with all boldness, while you stretch out your hand to heal, and signs and wonders are performed through the name of your holy servant Jesus." When they had prayed, the place in which they were gathered together was shaken; and they were all filled with the Holy Spirit and spoke the word of God with boldness. (Acts 4:29-31)

What would our prayer be in a similar situation? If imprisoned and commanded to speak no more of Jesus, would we pray for safety? Would we ask God to change the hearts of the officials? Would we ask for persecution to cease? The disciples ask for none of these. They pray for one thing: for boldness to speak God's word. They pray not for an easier path, but for the courage and power to walk the path Jesus walked.

And they are answered! The house shakes, the Spirit fills them, and they do speak with boldness. Today's church needs to be shaken. Today's church needs boldness. We face little persecution for our faith, yet our Christian witness is tentative and apologetic. We believe in Christ, but we don't want to "force that belief on others." Many Christians have bought into our culture's teaching that one faith is as good as another. We have abandoned, or at least apologize for, the exclusiveness of Christianity: that no other name but Jesus can save. We need courage to speak what we have seen and heard, to proclaim the good news of Jesus. We need the courage that comes only through prayer.

But the Father not only grants courage in persecution, he also can deliver us from evil. In Acts 12, Herod throws Peter in prison, intending to have him executed. Many disciples meet at the house of Mary, the mother of John Mark, to pray for Peter's release. God hears their prayer and sends an angel to free Peter. Peter then comes to Mary's house:

When he knocked at the outer gate, a maid named Rhoda came to answer. On recognizing Peter's voice, she was so overjoyed that, instead of opening the gate, she ran in and announced that Peter was standing at the gate. They said to her, "You are out of your mind!" But she insisted that it was so. They said, "It is his angel." Meanwhile Peter continued knocking; and when they opened the gate, they saw him and were amazed. He motioned to them with his hand to be silent, and described for them how he was brought out of the prison. (Acts 12:13-17)

The disciples's lack of faith is almost humorous. They are praying for Peter's release, but they don't believe it when he comes to their door. But they still had enough faith to pray, and God answered them more quickly than they could imagine.

This story illustrates the power of God and the power of prayer. God grants courage to those who are persecuted, but if he wills, he can remove the persecution. It is always right to pray "deliver us from evil," if we also pray "your will, not ours, be done." God miraculously delivers Peter and later delivers Paul and Silas from prison while they are "praying and singing hymns to God" (Acts 16:25-34). Prayer can do what seems impossible. At times we may be like the disciples at Mary's house, praying when the situation seems hopeless. But we must not fail to pray.

Yet God does not always set the prisoners free. He sometimes wills his followers to give the last full measure of their devotion. These martyrs, these witnesses to Jesus find strength and comfort in prayer, even at the point of death, just as Jesus himself prayed on the cross. While being stoned to death, Stephen prays the prayer of Jesus: "While they were stoning Stephen, he prayed, 'Lord Jesus, receive my spirit.' Then he knelt down and cried in a loud voice, 'Lord, do not hold this sin against them.' When he had said this he died" (Acts 7:59-60).

The early church was a suffering church. They counted it joy to suffer for Jesus. They prayed for boldness to witness, no matter what the cost. Some even gave their lives for Jesus, praying to him with their last breath.

The contemporary church, at least in America, is a satisfied church. Fat and happy, we cannot imagine the possibility of martyrdom. The great persecution we face today is embarrassed looks, caustic comments, and perhaps a cold shoulder or two. But these puny trials are often enough to keep us quiet about our faith.

Only through prayer can we capture the boldness of these early Christians. Only through prayer can we share their trust in a Father who delivers us from all opposition, even from death itself.

Questions for Further Discussion _____

1. What are some specific ways today's church can be devoted to prayer? Does your church have a prayer ministry? Shouldn't it? How can you organize one?

2. Does your church spend much time in prayer when selecting leaders? Do we choose our leaders or does Jesus? Who should?

3. Should we cast lots today? What keeps us from it, fear of superstition or lack of faith in God to answer?

4. Should we fast today? What place does laying on of hands have in your church? Should we revive these first-century practices?

5. What is more difficult, to believe God will free Christians in prison or to trust him when he does not release them?

Try This Week

Do a twenty-four hour fast from food one day this week. In that time focus on prayer for the leaders of your church.

A Book to Read

Roberta Bondi looks at early Christian prayer after the first century in *To Pray and to Love* (Minneapolis: Augsburg Fortress, 1991).

Chapter 17

"YOUR PRAYER HAS BEEN HEARD"
Prayer as Constant Trust

"Your prayers and your alms have ascended as a memorial before God."

ACTS 10:4

God gives good gifts. Jesus promised the Father would give the greatest gift, the Holy Spirit, to those who ask. "If you then, who are evil, know how to give good gifts to your children, how much more will the heavenly Father give the Holy Spirit to those who ask him!" (Luke 11:13).

The Giving of the Spirit
(Acts 8:14-17)

Prayer and the Holy Spirit are connected throughout the New Testament. At Jesus' baptism, the Spirit descends on him while he is praying. Through prayer, the Spirit works in selecting church leaders. Later, in the epistles, we will find the Spirit helps us when we pray, interceding with God for us. We are not surprised to find that Jesus' promise that God will send his Spirit is fulfilled in prayer:

Now when the apostles at Jerusalem heard that Samaria had accepted the word of God, they sent Peter and John to them. The two went down and prayed for them that they might receive the Holy Spirit (for as yet the Spirit had not come upon any of them; they had only been baptized in the name of the Lord Jesus). Then Peter and John laid their hands on them, and they received the Holy Spirit. (Acts 8:14-17)

The power to give the Holy Spirit was not in the apostles, but in God. Only after Peter and John prayed for them did the Samaritans receive the Spirit. We too can take Jesus at his word and pray that the Holy Spirit of God will live in us, guide us, and empower us. This is God's greatest gift because it is the Spirit who makes us children of God.

Prayer for Forgiveness
(Acts 8:18-24; 9:10-19)

Not everyone understood about the giving of the Spirit. While there is some mystery to the coming of the Spirit (like the wind, he "blows where he chooses," John 3:8), one man completely misunderstood the process. His name was Simon and, being a magician, he thought the Spirit came magically through Peter and John. Simon must not have grasped the role of prayer in the giving of the Spirit; it came from God, not humans. He offered money to Peter and John to buy this "magical" power:

But Peter said to him, "May your silver perish with you, because you thought you could obtain God's gift with money! You have no part or share in this, for your heart is not right before God. Repent therefore of this wickedness of yours, and pray to the Lord that, if possible, the intent of your heart may be forgiven you. For I see that you are in the gall of bitterness and the chains of wickedness." Simon answered, "Pray for me to the Lord, that nothing of what you have said may happen to me." (Acts 8:20-24)

He may not have understood the role of prayer in giving the Spirit, but Simon did understand Peter's threat and his call to repentance. Peter tells Simon to pray for forgiveness. Simon must have felt unworthy to do so; he asks Peter to pray to the Lord for him.

Saul is another who prays for forgiveness. He had blasphemed Jesus and murdered his followers. On the way to Damascus to capture more Christians, Saul is struck blind by a bright light and hears a voice from heaven, a voice that identifies itself as "Jesus, whom you are persecuting." He is told to go into the city and wait for instructions (Acts 8:1-9).

For three days he does not eat or drink. We are told, "he is praying" (Acts 8:11). We are not told what he prayed, but surely one thing was uppermost in his mind: the need for forgiveness. Saul had thought Jesus a fake, a false messiah who led people astray. Out of a mistaken zeal for God, he had imprisoned and killed those who spoke of Jesus' resurrection. Now he had heard the voice of the resurrected Christ. Now he knew himself not as a faithful crusader for God's truth, but as a murderer of the faithful, an enemy of the true Messiah sent by God. All that Saul had fought for was a lie. His life was upside down. No wonder he fasted and prayed. How could God hear the prayers of such a sinner?

But God heard and answered. Ananias came. Saul received his sight. He is baptized, "calling on the name of the Lord" (Acts 22:16). He is filled with the Holy Spirit (Acts 9:17).

If God hears the pleas of sinners like Simon and Saul, then he hears our cries for mercy. Although Saul, later known as Paul, calls himself the chief of sinners, we know better. We know our own sins. We may not try to buy the Spirit, and we may not kill those who witness to Jesus, but we know our own need for forgiveness. Like Simon and Saul, we too pray the tax collector's prayer, "Lord, be merciful to me, a sinner." And like the tax collector, we go away justified, forgiven by our gracious God.

Prayer for Healing
(Acts 9:40; 28:7-10)

"It's a miracle!"

Such a phrase scares many of us today. We have seen too many fake miracle workers. Although we are Christians, we may think that God worked only in the past and now works only through "natural law." But the same God who worked in Jesus through prayer also worked in the apostles. He's the same God who works his mighty power in us today.

Jesus had promised power to the apostles, power through the Spirit that enabled them to do "many wonders and signs" (Acts 2:43). In the Gospels, these same apostles had trusted their own power and so were unable to heal the boy with a demon (Mark 9:18). In Acts, they have learned the lesson Jesus taught them: "This kind can come out only through prayer" (Mark 9:29). Through the power of God, the apostles perform the same miracles Jesus performed. They can even raise the dead! When a loving disciple named Tabitha (or Dorcas) dies, the church calls for Peter, who raises her from the dead. But like Jesus at Lazarus' tomb, he does so only through prayer:

> Peter put all of them outside, and then he knelt down and prayed. He turned to the body and said, "Tabitha, get up." Then she opened her eyes, and seeing Peter, she sat up. He gave her his hand and helped her up. Then calling the saints and widows, he showed her to be alive. This became known throughout Joppa, and many believed in the Lord. (Acts 9:40-43)

Through prayer the ultimate healing takes place. Dorcas is raised from the dead. As with Lazarus, her resurrection leads many to believe.

Other healings took place through prayer. Paul, like Peter, performs miracles similar to those of Jesus: "It so happened that the father of Publius lay sick in bed with fever and dysentery. Paul visited him and cured him by praying and putting his hands on him. After this happened, the rest of the people on the island who had diseases also came and were cured" (Acts 28:8-9).

Acts makes it clear that healing took place in prayer. Today we have no one with the power of a Peter or a Paul, but we still pray for healing, and we still have the power that was in Peter and Paul: the power of Jesus. When doctors pronounce a case hopeless, Christians are reluctant to pray for healing. But we must not doubt the power and goodness of God. When all is hopeless, God can heal.

However, prayer is much more than a last resort. If we pray only when things are hopeless, we miss the point of prayer. Prayer is not magic. God is powerful; he can heal. God is good; he wants to heal. But God is also God. He alone is the sovereign ruler of the universe. His will, not ours, must guide us.

Dorcas is raised from the dead; Stephen is not. Publius' father is instantly healed of sickness; Paul (who healed him) is himself not healed of his thorn in the flesh. Peter is released from prison; James is not, and is beheaded. Acts is not the story of a constantly triumphant church. Prayer is not a sure formula for health, wealth, and success. Yes, we should pray in faith for healing, but we pray that God's will be done. When we are healed, it is by his power. When we are not, it is still his power through prayer that sustains us.

Acts is careful to make the point that healing power comes from Jesus, not from the apostles themselves. Today, some who claim to heal forget the power is God's. But though there are as many "fake healers" as "faith healers," we must not let our cynicism keep us from praying to the true source of health: our Father in heaven.

Prayer for Guidance
(Acts 10:1-16, 31, 34-48; 22:17-21)

"Does God hear the prayer of a sinner?" I certainly hope so! All of us are sinners. God hears and forgives us when we pray. "But does God hear the prayer of one who is not a Christian?" Certainly not, if that person has finally rejected Christ. If one rejects Jesus, how can one pray in his name? "But what about the person who wants to do right, to follow Jesus, but does not know how?"

Ah, that's different. There are many in our world who have some idea of God, but do not know Jesus. There may even be some in "Christian" America who know of Jesus and his church, but are confused as to how to follow him. What should such a person do?

There is such a person in Acts. His name is Cornelius. What he does is pray for guidance:

> In Caesarea there was a man named Cornelius, a centurion of the Italian cohort, as it was called. He was a devout man who feared God with all his household; he gave alms generously to the people and prayed constantly to God. One afternoon at about three o'clock he had a vision in which he clearly saw an angel of God coming in and saying to him, "Cornelius." He stared at him in terror and said, "What is it, Lord?" He answered, "Your prayers and your alms have ascended as a memorial before God. Now send men to Joppa for a certain Simon who is called Peter; he is lodging with Simon, a tanner, whose house is by the seaside." (Acts 10:1-6)

God definitely hears Cornelius' prayers (Acts 10:30). Cornelius sends for Peter whom God has prepared through a vision (Acts 10:9-16). Peter arrives, preaches the gospel to Cornelius and his family, the Spirit falls upon them, and they are baptized (Acts 10:34-48). God hears the prayers of all who seek him. If we do not know how to walk with God, we should pray for guidance. God might not send a Peter, but in some way he will show us how to serve him. This is true not only for non-Christians, but for believers also. Even the most committed disciples have times when they don't know how to love Christ. None understands the way of God perfectly. We come to know his will through Scripture and prayer.

Sometimes our question is not, "How can I serve God," but simply, "What do I do now?" Life is full of decisions, great and small, and in those decisions we must seek the guidance of the Lord. After his conversion, Saul returns to Jerusalem and receives such guidance:

> "After I had returned to Jerusalem and while I was praying in the temple, I fell into a trance and saw Jesus saying to me, 'Hurry and get out of Jerusalem quickly, because they will not accept your testimony about me.' And I said, 'Lord, they themselves know that in every synagogue I imprisoned and beat those who believed in you. And while the blood of your witness Stephen was shed, I myself was standing by and keeping the coats of those who killed him.' Then he said to me, 'Go, for I will send you far away to the Gentiles.'" (Acts 22:17-21)

This is an important turning point in Paul's life. He wants to stay in Jerusalem and clear his name. He wants his old friends to know that he now follows this Jesus whom he once persecuted. But Jesus has other plans for Saul. He wants to send him to the Gentiles. In prayer, Paul hears Jesus say, "Go."

Like Paul, we too make our plans. We decide where to live, what job to have, how to spend our time. Like Paul, we may wish to stay when Jesus says go. But Paul heard the voice of Jesus in prayer, and he obeyed. Prayer is not just speaking, it is listening.

Paul may not be a perfect example for us here. I'm not convinced we should fall into a trance when we pray. I'm not sure exactly how Jesus speaks to us in prayer. I myself have never heard an audible voice, but wrestling with a decision in prayer, I believe he has answered me and guided me. Sometimes, like Paul, his answer is not what I want to hear, but if we ask God for advice, we better be prepared to take it.

Jesus did not leave the church alone. He has not left us alone. If we want to know his will, we read his word, the Bible. We follow the example of his body, the church. And we seek his voice in the silence of prayer. We are not alone. He guides our lives.

Prayer When Parting
(Acts 20:36-38; 21:4-6)

Prayer is not always just between our Father and us. We sometimes pray with our fellow travelers in God's way. Prayer with other Christians is touching and appropriate when we part from them. Having left Ephesus after spending two years there, Paul returns to Miletus on his way to Jerusalem. From there he sends for the elders of the Ephesian church, seeing them for what he thinks will be the last time:

> "When he had finished speaking, he knelt down with them all and prayed. There was much weeping among them all; they embraced Paul and kissed him, grieving especially because of what he had said, that they would not see him again. Then they brought him to the ship" (Acts 20:36-38).

What a heartrending prayer this must have been! Just a few days later, Paul repeats this scene with the Christians at Tyre (Acts 21:5-6). Like Paul, we know the church is a family. To leave fellow Christians is not just parting from friends; it's more like leaving home. But what makes us family is a common Father. In prayer we are united with the Father and with each other. No doubt Paul and the Ephesians prayed that God would protect them. No doubt they prayed to be reunited in heaven, their true home. But in the very act of parting, they were one in prayer. Nothing can part us from our Christian brothers and sisters. No matter how far away from us they be, in this world or the next, we are one with them in prayer.

A Praying Church

In many ways the church in Acts is a model church. However, these early Christians were not perfect. They bickered and fought. Their faith wavered. There were hypocrites in their midst. But most of them held firmly to their faith, even in the face of persecution. They were devoted to God and to one another. Most of all, they were a praying church, calling on their Father time and time again for courage, forgiveness, and guidance. If we are to imitate their faith, we too are called to be praying Christians, completely dependent on God through Christ.

What makes for a good church today? Is the best church the one with the most dynamic preacher? The most programs? The largest attendance? Do we measure a church by the excitement of its members? By the size of its parking lot? By its reputation?

No. The truest measure of a church is its devotion to God. Nothing reflects that devotion more than prayer. If we lack the spirituality and power of the early church, perhaps our prayer life is the first thing we should change.

Questions for Further Discussion

1. Should we pray today to receive the Holy Spirit? How do we know that the Spirit is with us?

2. Is there any sin God will not forgive? What is the relationship among repentance, prayer, and forgiveness?

3. What makes us nervous about praying for healing? Do you think God heals "miraculously" today? If not, why should we pray for the sick?

4. Have you ever prayed with someone when you part from them? What did you pray for?

5. What more can your church do to show it believes in the healing and forgiving power of prayer?

Try This Week

Focus your prayers this week on those you love who are far away from you. Pray in faith that they are safe in God's hands and that they are praying for you.

A Book to Read

Andrew Murray's classic on intercession from 1897 has been recently republished as *The Ministry of Intercession: Training for Prayer Warriors* (CreateSpace, 2009).

Chapter 18

"I Thank God for You"
Prayer as Relationship with God's People

"First, I thank my God through Jesus Christ for all of you."

ROMANS 1:8

In reading Paul's epistles many Christians skip over his prayers to get to the "good stuff." For some the good part is Paul's deep presentation of Christian doctrine. His letters are full of profound teachings on redemption, the Holy Spirit, the resurrection, and other doctrines.

For some the good stuff is Paul's advice on Christian living, his comforting words on love, joy, and peace. Paul's letters are indeed a deep reservoir of guidance on Christian living and doctrine, but we can miss both the beauty of discipleship and the significance of doctrine if we ignore his prayers.

When Paul writes a church he begins by praying for them. This is more than a mere custom of letter composition; by praying Paul recognizes God the Father and the Lord Jesus as the true correspondents with the church. Their power called the church into existence. Their love binds the church together. Their Spirit gives the church life.

Moreover, Paul's prayers usually set the themes for his letters. If you want to know what concerns, frightens, and encourages him about a church, look first to his prayers. There you will find what is on his heart.

By looking at Paul's prayers for the churches, we too can learn to pray for our brothers and sisters in Christ, for those in our local congregation, in other churches, and even those far away whom we have never met.

For the Romans
(Romans 1:8-12)

Though he knew many in their number, Paul had never visited the church at Rome. This was not a church he had planted, so one might expect his letter to them to show less depth of feeling than his other letters. But that is certainly not the case:

> First, I thank my God through Jesus Christ for all of you, because your faith is proclaimed throughout the world. For God, whom I serve with my spirit by announcing the gospel of his Son, is my witness that without ceasing I remember you always in my prayers, asking that by God's will I may somehow at last succeed in coming to you. For I am longing to see you so that I may share with you some spiritual gift to strengthen you - or rather so that we may be mutually encouraged by each other's faith, both yours and mine. (Romans 1:8-12)

Paul's warm affection for the Romans stems from his knowledge of their faith. So faithful were they that the whole world proclaimed it. Paul prays for them constantly, asking God to bring him to visit them in Rome. The great apostle wants to bring them a spiritual gift, but he also longs to be strengthened by their world-renowned faith.

Much can be learned from Paul's brief prayer for the Romans. He could have stressed his own authority as an apostle, his power to heal and pass on spiritual gifts. Indeed, he does mention his call to be an apostle, but in his prayer he prays for mutual encouragement. Paul had learned what truly spiritual disciples always know: no matter how mature in Christ one becomes, one always needs encouragement from faithful Christians. Paul certainly knew discouragement; he had endured beatings, stonings, and shipwreck. But when he thought of these faithful Romans, resolute even in adversity, his spirits were brightened.

We may not face persecution as Christians, but we do face discouragement. Even (perhaps especially) those who publicly lead the church face disappointment and heartbreak. But those of us who lead and teach know that we receive more than we give to our congregations. The examples of ordinary, quiet, but faithful Christians convinces us anew of the truth and power of our faith.

Margaret is such a Christian. A widow, retired from a career in college teaching, her health is somewhat fragile. She cannot see very well after dark, yet she never misses a church service, even though at times she has to get another church member to drive her. If you were to visit our church, you probably wouldn't notice her; she isn't loud and boisterous but her acts of quiet service, known only to a few, do not go unnoticed by God.

There are many Margarets in our church and in yours. Such Christians keep my faith alive. Like Paul, I long to meet more of them. Like Paul, we all should pray for opportunities to meet Christian brothers and sisters who will strengthen our faith as we strengthen theirs.

For the Corinthians
(1 Corinthians 1:4-9; 2 Corinthians 1:3-7; 13:7-10)

Was there ever a church as mixed-up as the Corinthians? They were proud of their sexual immorality. They were split into quarrelling factions. They sued each other in pagan courtrooms. They got drunk during the Lord's Supper. They bragged about their spiritual gifts, but did not know the way of love.

In short, if there ever was an apostate church it was Corinth. How disappointed Paul must have been when he thought of them. He had founded the church at Corinth and spent a year and a half there trying to shape them into disciples of Jesus. As soon as he left, other teachers arrived claiming to know more than Paul and ridiculing his authority. The Corinthians followed these "super-apostles" quite readily.

How do you pray for a church like Corinth? My first inclination would be to pray God to pay them in kind, to blast them out of the water as they deserve. That is not Paul's prayer. With all their faults, the Corinthians had received the grace of God. His prayer for them is not one of rebuke, but of thanksgiving:

I give thanks to my God always for you because of the grace of God that has been given you in Christ Jesus, for in every way you have been enriched in him, in speech and knowledge of every kind—just as the testimony of Christ has been strengthened among you—so that you are not lacking in any spiritual gift as you wait for the revealing of our Lord Jesus Christ. He will also strengthen you to the end, so that you may be blameless on the day of our Lord Jesus Christ. God is faithful; by him you were called into the fellowship of his Son, Jesus Christ our Lord. (1 Corinthians 1:4-9)

Thank God the salvation of the Corinthians was not dependent on their ability to be a model church, but on God's gracious act in Jesus Christ. This gracious God gave them their spiritual gifts—faith and knowledge. This faithful God will present them blameless at the last day.

This does not mean the Corinthians had no reason to repent; in the rest of Corinthians Paul enumerates their shortcomings and calls them back to faithfulness. They must put away selfish divisions; they must have orderly worship; they must live moral lives based on love. But all these things are by God's grace alone, and for that grace Paul is thankful.

How do we pray for the weak, apostate Christian? We may be tempted to pray, "Lord, straighten them out!" There is a place for such a prayer. Our brothers and sisters may need God to figuratively hit them between the eyes to get their attention. But in praying for wayward Christians, remember that no matter how sinful they are, they are our brother or sister in Christ. They too are saved by God's grace, as are we, and it is that grace that calls them to repentance. Even the worst Christian can be an occasion to thank God for his marvelous grace.

The tone of 2 Corinthians differs greatly from that of 1 Corinthians. It appears the Corinthians have repented of many of the wrongs they had committed, so Paul prays God will console them:

Blessed be the Father of our Lord Jesus Christ, the Father of mercies and the God of all consolation, who consoles us in all our affliction, so that we may be able to console those who are in any affliction with the consolation with which we ourselves are consoled by God. For just as the sufferings of Christ are abundant for us, so also our consolation is abundant through Christ. If we are afflicted, it is for your consolation and salvation; if we are being consoled, it is for your consolation, which you experience when you patiently endure the same sufferings that we are also suffering. Our hope for you is unshaken; for we know that as you share in our sufferings, so also you share in our consolation. (2 Corinthians 1:3-7)

Talk about repeating yourself, Paul uses the word consolation nine times in these five verses. Why did the Corinthians need to be comforted? One reason was their sorrow for their sins. Paul had written them a harsh letter, calling the sincerity of their faith into question. Even in this letter he urges them to test their faith to see if it is genuine (2 Corinthians 13:5). When confronted by sin, the faithful Christian responds with a godly sorrow that leads to repentance. This is more than merely saying you're sorry; to repent is to realize one has offended the holy God and has hurt Jesus himself, the one who died for us. Such sorrow cuts deep into the soul and can only be removed by the consolation of God's forgiveness.

The Corinthians also needed consolation in affliction. If there was anyone who knew suffering and pain, it was Paul. If there was anyone who knew the comfort of God in the midst of pain, it was Paul. As the Father comforted the Son in his agony, so he consoled Paul who in turn shared the comfort of God with the Corinthians.

I have not faced much physical affliction for my faith, but I have known sickness, pain, and injury. Several years ago, I broke my elbow. I'd like to claim some noble reason for my pain, but the fact is I broke it playing softball. For the three weeks my right arm was in a cast, I couldn't write, mow the grass, or even feed myself easily. During this time, the church gave me a surprise birthday party, and one brother endeared himself to me forever by cutting my cake into bite-sized pieces. Such was my "great suffering." But as minor as it was, I needed consolation from my fellow Christians and from God, and I got it. In troubles small and great, God is our consolation, and he expects us to console others.

Most of our suffering is not a result of our Christian faith. Suffering for Christ seems far removed from our experience as Christians. Once being a good church member advanced, not hindered, our standing in the wider community. But the times they are changing. We no longer live in a Christian America. In most places, being a dedicated Christian will not help you socially or on the job. For most in our society, Christianity is still tolerable "as long as you don't take it too far." But that is precisely what we are called to do, to go too far, to give our all to Christ. No, we don't have to be objectionable just to be so, but if we have the mind of Christ and strive to live his life, some will object, perhaps even violently. We too may come to know the need for God's comfort in persecution.

We also need comfort when facing loss. I remember a funeral early in my ministry. Russell Cooper had been a faithful leader in our church. A few years before his death, he had a series of strokes that left him severely incapacitated. Each day for years his wife Myrtie faithfully visited Russell in the nursing home and cared for him. She consoled him with God's consolation. Russell passed away and I was asked to read Scripture and pray at his funeral. Ostensibly I was there to comfort Myrtie, but her example of giving, undying love was the true consolation to all around her.

The Corinthians had lost loved ones, too. Some were beginning to doubt the resurrection. They thought they would never see their loved ones again. In 1 Corinthians 15 Paul had written them to assure them that death would be swallowed up in victory. As we stood by Russell's grave, I thought of those comforting words.

Suffering, sin, and death—three strong foes of faith. Paul knew the Corinthians could crack under their pressure, so at the end of this letter he says another prayer for them, a prayer for their perfection:

> But we pray to God that you may not do anything wrong—not that we may appear to have met the test, but that you may do what is right, though we may seem to have failed. For we cannot do anything against the truth, but only for the truth. For we rejoice when we are weak and you are strong. This is what we pray for that you may become perfect. So I write these things while I am away from you, so that when I come, I may not have to be severe in using the authority that the Lord has given me for building up and not for tearing down. (2 Corinthians 13:7-10)

Paul's final words sound ominous, but in the context of prayer we find their true intent. Paul is not an authoritarian dictator but a loving father in the gospel. Even if he fails, he wants the Corinthians to pass the test of faith, so he calls on the only power that can make them pass. He calls on God in prayer.

Suffering, sin, and death are our foes too, along with indifference, materialism, and pride. If our faith is to pass the test, we also must rely on God in prayer. And we must pray for each other. If Paul could ask God to perfect a church as weak as Corinth, then we can pray for our weakest brother or sister. And they can pray for us.

For the Ephesians
(Ephesians 1:16-19; 3:14-19)

Knowledge is power. At least that is what we are told in today's information age. When writing the Ephesians, Paul prays they will receive a different sort of knowledge and power:

> I do not cease to give thanks for you as I remember you in my prayers. I pray that the Father of our Lord Jesus Christ, the Father of glory, may give you a spirit of wisdom and revelation as you come to know him, so that, with the eyes of your heart enlightened, you may know what is the hope to which he has called you, what are the riches of his glorious inheritance among the saints, and what is the immeasurable greatness of his power for us who believe, according to the working of his great power. (Ephesians 1:16-19)

Knowledge of God is much more than a theological education. I do not want to disparage Christian education—I've been in that business all my life—but knowing *about* God is not the same as knowing God. Knowing the Bible is important. We should teach it to our children, take time to study it ourselves, and insist our ministers get the best biblical education they can get. But book knowledge, even of the best Book, is not the same as knowing someone. God surely wants us to learn about him, but most of all he wants us to know him.

I know many things about my wife Deb: her taste in clothes, her favorite color, the foods she likes, her sense of humor. But passing a quiz on her tastes and habits does not qualify me as a good husband or insure a good marriage. What makes our marriage good is that we know one another. We are part of each other. We think and feel together. God calls us to have this same kind of intimate knowledge of him. Paul prays the Ephesians will receive not simply intellectual information, but that "the eyes of your heart may be enlightened." Our Father wants us to see him with the eyes of our heart. Can there be a more intimate knowledge?

Such knowledge is a gift of God. Yes, we must strain every nerve to know our Father, but we can only know him as he reveals himself to us. Paul prays that God "may give you a spirit of wisdom and revelation so that you may know him better." If we want to know God better, we need only to ask him. Do you want to improve your Bible study? Then coat your studies with prayer. Knowledge comes through prayer. In prayer we come to know the Father intimately, and in prayer he grants us even fuller knowledge.

Who is this God we come to know? He is the God who gives hope, "the riches of his glorious inheritance in the saints." The more we come to know him the more we come to realize what he has done for us. When we were hopeless, he gave us hope. When we were orphans, he adopted us and made us heirs. Today our world is low on hope. Cynicism abounds. The things on which we place our hope prove futile: wealth, technology, democracy, family, pleasure, and others. God alone is the source of true hope. His is a true and sure hope, not just a fond wish for things to get better. The more we come to know our Father, the clearer we see the reality of our inheritance. We have begun to live with him forever.

Knowledge is power. The God we come to know is a powerful God. The same power that raised Christ from the dead, that placed him in the heavens, that appointed him head over the church, that same power is at work in us (Ephesians 1:20-23). To know God is to have power over temptation, sin, evil, and Satan. To know God is to have power over every situation we face each day. To know God is to have the power of Christ in us, the Christ who fills us in every way.

Knowledge is power. Paul repeats that in his second prayer for the Ephesians:

For this reason I bow my knees before the Father, from whom every family in heaven and on earth takes its name. I pray that, according to the riches of his glory, he may grant that you may be strengthened in your inner being with power through his Spirit, and that Christ may dwell in your hearts through faith, as you are being rooted and grounded in love. I pray that you may have the power to comprehend, with all the saints, what is the breadth and length and height and depth, and to know the love of Christ that surpasses knowledge, so that you may be filled with all the fullness of God. (Ephesians 3:14-19)

Knowledge of God brings power, but here Paul turns it around: he prays the Ephesians will have the power to know. To know what? To know the essence of Christ, the extent of his love. Yet that love is beyond knowledge. We can't imagine how wide and long and high and deep it is. But as we come to know our God and our Christ, we grasp more and more the love they are. That love fills us and spills from us to all we meet.

Do you want to know God? Then pray. Ask to know him. Do you sometimes feel hopeless? Then pray. Ask to know the sure hope to which he calls us. Are you sometimes powerless against the forces arrayed against you? Pray for power. Power to overcome. Power to know the love of Christ. Do not face your problems on your own. Power is yours. All you have to do is ask.

Questions for Further Discussion

1. Do you often pray for other Christians to be encouraged? Do you ask them to pray for your own encouragement? Isn't this as legitimate a prayer request as praying for the sick?

2. Should we pray for weak Christians? What should our prayer be for them? Is there a temptation to feel superior to them?

3. Think of some situations when you needed comfort from God and fellow Christians. Have you prayed lately for others in a similar situation? What is the best way we can comfort others?

4. Can Christians be perfect? What do we mean by "perfect"? What does the Bible mean by it? Should we pray that others might be perfect?

5. How are prayer and Bible study related? How do we come to know God in prayer? What do we want to know about him? How does knowledge bring power?

Try This Week

Think of someone you know who needs encouragement. This week, pray each day that God will comfort and strengthen him or her.

A Book to Read

For a daily prayer book that touches various circumstances of life, use Germaine Copeland, *Prayers that Avail Much* (Tulsa: Harrison House, 1997).

Chapter 19

"WE HAVE NOT CEASED PRAYING FOR YOU"
Prayer as Desire for Holiness

"We have not ceased praying for you and asking that
you may be filled with the knowledge of God's will."

COLOSSIANS 1:9

What I'm about to say may shock you, especially those of you who have been in church all of your life. But it's the truth and I must say it: I've never been part of a bad church. Every church I've experienced has been full of people who give of themselves fully and freely, who show love to the downtrodden, and who express the true joy of God. Oh sure, there have been exceptional church members who gossip, lie, and cheat, but they have been rare in my church experience.

So how do you pray for a good church? What do you say about Christians whose lives seem much more exemplary than your own? Paul knew such a church, and he knew how to pray for them.

For the Philippians
(Philippians 1:3-6, 9-11)

Every church has its problems and its strong points, but if there is one church in the New Testament that can be described as a model church, it is the church at

Philippi. When Paul writes the Philippians, the tone of his letter is completely positive with lavish praise for them. This tone is set in his prayer for the Philippians:

> I thank my God every time I remember you, constantly praying with joy
> in every one of my prayers for all of you, because of your sharing in the
> gospel from the first day until now. I am confident of this, that the one who
> began a good work among you will bring it to completion by the day of Jesus
> Christ.... And this is my prayer, that your love may overflow more and more
> with knowledge and full insight to help you determine what is best, so that
> in the day of Christ you may be pure and blameless, having produced the
> harvest of righteousness that comes through Jesus Christ for the glory and
> praise of God. (Philippians 1:3-6, 9-11)

Paul's prayers for the Philippians are prayers of joy. Joy and rejoicing are central themes in this letter. Paul introduces these themes in his prayer. What is it about the Philippians that makes Paul rejoice? Their sharing in the gospel. The Philippians had gladly received the gospel as the saving truth from God. More than that, they had supported Paul's proclamation of the gospel through their generous gifts and their prayers. Yet this good work was not their own doing; Christ began it, and Paul prays he will bring it to completion at the last day.

Paul's prayer for the Philippians is quite similar to his prayer for the Corinthians and the Ephesians. As with the Ephesians, he wants God to grant them love and knowledge. Paul wanted the Ephesians to know the love of God; he wants the Philippians' love to overflow with knowledge. In Christianity, love and knowledge go hand in hand. To know God is to love him. If we love him, we come to know him more and more.

This knowledge of God is more than simply an intellectual achievement. Knowing God changes the way we think, the way we live, the way we treat others. As Paul prayed for the Corinthians, so he prays for the Philippians that this God they have come to know and love will produce good lives—a "harvest of righteousness"—so that they may be pure and blameless on the day of Christ.

Is this the way we pray for our fellow Christians? It seems most of our prayers are for people to be healed or comforted. There is nothing wrong with those prayers; Paul also prayed for his brothers and sisters to be healed or consoled, but he was primarily concerned with their standing before God. From Paul the church today can learn to pray for what is most important: that we and our fellow Christians may know the love of God and may live blameless lives, looking forward to that final, endless day of Jesus Christ.

For the Colossians
(Colossians 1:3-5, 9-12)

It is not surprising for Paul to repeat himself in his prayers for the different churches. After all, most churches are similar, facing the same struggles and sharing the same joys. We must remember that these are not Paul's actual prayers, but his reports of his prayers. If we could hear Paul pray for the churches, we would no doubt find his prayers personalized to fit each congregation.

When we come to Paul's prayer for the Colossian church, we find little that is new. Colossians was written about the same time as Ephesians and the two letters are quite similar. Paul's prayer for the Colossians thus echoes many of the themes of his other prayers:

> In our prayers for you we always thank God, the Father of our Lord Jesus Christ, for we have heard of your faith in Christ Jesus and of the love that you have for all the saints, because of the hope laid up for you in heaven.
>
> For this reason, since the day we heard it, we have not ceased praying for you and asking that you may be filled with the knowledge of God's will in all spiritual wisdom and understanding, so that you may lead lives worthy of the Lord, fully pleasing to him, as you bear fruit in every good work and as you grow in the knowledge of God. May you be strong with all the strength that comes from his glorious power, and may you be prepared to endure everything with patience, while joyfully giving thanks to the Father, who has enabled you to share in the inheritance of the saints in the light. (Colossians 1:3-5, 9-12)

Here is Paul's usual prayer vocabulary. He thanks God for their faith, hope, and love, and prays for them to receive the knowledge that brings good works, strength, and endurance. The new terms he emphasizes in Colossians are hope and endurance, perhaps reflecting the sufferings of the church or of Paul himself, since he wrote this from prison (Colossians 4:10). In either case, endurance is needed. The power to endure springs from one of the greatest doctrines of Christianity: the hope laid up for us in heaven.

The Bible's definition of hope is the complete opposite of the way we usually use the word. In everyday use, to hope is to wish fondly for something—"I hope it doesn't rain today," "I hope the boss gives me a raise," "I hope little Johnny is all right,"— wishes with varying degrees of certainty about their outcome. In the Scriptures hope is a sure thing, because it is based not on our own actions, but on the gracious act of God in Jesus Christ.

Growing up as a Christian, I remember several occasions when older Christians were asked, "If you died today, would you go to heaven?" Almost invariably they answered, "I hope so," in much the same tone they used to say, "I hope it doesn't rain today." The one exception was an elderly woman in our church who promptly replied, "Yes, I know I'd go to heaven." When asked how she could be so sure, she said simply, "God told me I was saved and I believe him." That lady knew the true meaning of Christian hope. Did not Christ say, "I go to prepare a place for you?" Didn't he pray that we should share his glory? If we believe him, our hope is sure.

But the hope of heaven is much more than pie in the sky when you die by and by. Our hope is laid up for us in heaven, but it also guides our present lives. Some fear assurance of salvation and certainty of hope will lead Christians to neglect their Christian duties; if we already have it made, why work for it? Paul sees hope in a different light. He thanks God for the Colossian's hope because it motivates their faith in Christ and their love for the saints. Hope in their inheritance gives them power to endure. Certainty of hope moves Christians to loving action for God and neighbor.

What has all of this to do with prayer? We too should thank God for the hope within us and the hope we see in fellow Christians. What is more, hope forms the context for every prayer we pray. We could not pray without hope of being heard. We could not pray, "Your will be done," if we had no sure hope that God's will would ultimately triumph. We always pray with confidence. So we always pray in hope.

For the Thessalonians
(I Thessalonians 1:2-3; 3:9-13; 2 Thessalonians 1:3, 11-12)

The Thessalonian letters are probably the earliest letters of Paul, yet they already contain his distinctive prayer vocabulary: "We always give thanks to God for all of you and mention you in our prayers, constantly remembering before our God and Father your work of faith and labor of love and steadfastness of hope in our Lord Jesus Christ" (1 Thessalonians 1:2-3).

Faith, hope, love—Paul's three favorite words. This is what he thanks God for. But these are more than theological terms for Paul, more than just church words to be used on Sunday. They are action words. He thanks God for their work of faith. True faith always shows itself in action, in work for God and neighbor. Paul thanks God for their labor of love. Love is no good if it is love in name only. Love must express itself in work for others. Paul thanks God for their steadfastness of hope. Here is no mere wishful thinking, but a sure hope that inspires endurance. To Paul, faith, hope, and love are not simply theological virtues; they always lead to ethical action. They are gifts from God and causes for thanksgiving.

Later in Thessalonians we have both an account of Paul's prayers for them and one of those prayers:

> How can we thank God enough for you in return for all the joy that we feel before our God because of you? Night and day we pray most earnestly that we may see you face to face and restore what ever is lacking in your faith.
>
> Now may our God and Father himself and our Lord Jesus direct our way to you. And may the Lord make you increase and abound in love for one another and for all, just as we abound in love for you. And may he so strengthen your hearts in holiness that you may be blameless before our God and Father at the coming of our Lord Jesus with all his saints. (1 Thessalonians 3:9-13)

Paul is so overwhelmed with the joy he feels when he thinks of the Thessalonians, that he breaks out in blessing. Thankful to God for that joy, he asks him to increase their love and to make them holy and blameless.

How often do we pray for holiness today? "Holiness" carries overtones of hypocrisy or fanaticism, but it is an essential biblical word that we should work to recover. To be genuinely holy is not to be "holier than thou" but rather to be transformed into the image of Christ. Holiness is no option for Christians; we must be holy to stand blameless before God at the coming of Jesus. But holiness is not the result of our own spiritual fervor or discipline; it is a gift of God. A gift to be sought in prayer. It is God who sanctifies us, who disciplines us, and who presents us blameless. As Paul prayed for the Thessalonians, so we should pray for God to strengthen our hearts in holiness.

Paul repeats his thanksgiving and requests for the church in 2 Thessalonians:

> We must always give thanks to God for you, brothers and sisters, as is right, because your faith is growing abundantly, and the love of everyone of you for one another is increasing.
>
> To this end we always pray for you, asking that our God will make you worthy of his call and will fulfill by his power every good resolve and work of faith, so that the name of our Lord Jesus may be glorified in you, and you in him, according to the grace of our God and the Lord Jesus Christ. (2 Thessalonians 1:3, 11-12)

Again he is thankful for their faith and prays God will empower their work of faith. He also prays God will make them worthy of his call. Here is a look backward and a look forward. We Christians look back to the moment God called us from a life of sin and we obeyed that call (2 Thessalonians 2:13-14). At that moment no one was worthy; we all were sinners without hope, yet God called us to eternal life. Thus we look forward to the coming of our Lord (2 Thessalonians 1:10). Between the time of our calling and the time of our glory, God works in us to make us worthy of his call. For that we pray.

For Timothy
(2 Timothy 1:3-5)

Gratitude for his fellow Christians marked Paul's life, and he is especially thankful for Timothy, his son in the faith. Paul calls him "my beloved child" and says:

> I am grateful to God—whom I worship with a clear conscience, as my ancestors did—when I remember you constantly in my prayers night and day. Recalling your tears, I long to see you so that I may be filled with joy. I am reminded of your sincere faith, a faith that lived first in your grandmother Lois and your mother Eunice and now, I am sure, lives in you. (2 Timothy 1:3-5)

Since Timothy's father was Greek (and by implication an unbeliever), Paul became Timothy's surrogate father. Timothy is blessed by two strong women in his life, Lois and Eunice, who taught him to have faith in God. Paul is thankful for these women, and thankful for Timothy's love for them and him. Timothy's tears stand as a witness of his love for Paul.

"Faith of our fathers, holy faith," we sometimes sing. But what about the faith of our mothers? For Timothy and for many of us, it was a faithful mother or grandmother who first taught us of Jesus. Some of my earliest memories are of mom tucking me into bed and reading me a Bible story. Few of us come to faith on our own; our families nurture our faith, sometimes through great effort and sacrifice.

We too have the duty and the honor of ensuring our children will have faith. To possess a faithful mother, grandmother, father, brother, sister, and child is a great boon from God. In prayer we, like Paul, thank him for those whose lives bless ours.

For Philemon
(Philemon 1:4-7)

This faith we have from our families is not a precious commodity to be hoarded. It is a precious commodity that should be shared. Paul writes Philemon and rejoices that he shares his faith with others:

> When I remember you in my prayers, I always thank my God because I hear of your love for all the saints and your faith toward the Lord Jesus. I pray that the sharing of your faith may become effective when you perceive all the good that we do for Christ. I have indeed received much joy and encouragement from your love, because the hearts of the saints have been refreshed through you, my brother. (Philemon 1:4-7)

Sharing your faith usually means evangelism, and that is probably what Paul has in mind here. However, we also share our faith with fellow Christians, refreshing their hearts. To share faith also means to do good for Christ. In Philemon's case, doing good meant receiving and forgiving Onesimus, his runaway slave.

Share the faith. This brief phrase summarizes the whole of the Christian life. If our faith is genuine, we will tell others the good news of Jesus. Our faith will encourage the hearts of the faithful. Our faith will lead us to good works, even to accept and forgive those who have wronged us. We thank God for our faith and the faith of others, and we pray for courage to share that faith.

Praying with Paul

What can we learn from Paul's prayers for the churches? First, we see Paul constantly in prayer. Like Jesus, he had a habit of prayer. We too must make prayer a regular part of our lives. Prayer is not just for church time, for meals, or at bedtime. Prayer is for all times and anytime.

Second, Paul prayed for others. The biblical word for this is intercession, a word we do not often use. But Christians desperately need our prayers and we need theirs. Paul realized he needed the prayers of the churches; he asked for their prayers. Let's not be too proud to ask our brothers and sisters to pray for us or get so wrapped up in our own concerns that we forget the needs of others. In Christ, we are all in this thing together; we need help; we need to pray.

Third, Paul's requests to God for the churches are usually spiritual matters. He rarely thanks God for their health or wealth, but he is thankful for their faith, hope, and love. He seldom asks God to bless them with the ordinary blessings of life, but he does pray God to give them spiritual discernment, steadfastness, and power. It is not wrong to ask for health or daily bread, but Paul knew what was really of value.

Finally, Paul told his readers that he was praying for them. In those rough weeks when everything goes wrong, our faith is tested, and we hover on the edge of despair, how marvelous it is to hear someone say, "I am praying for you." We should not only pray for our brothers and sisters in Christ, we should encourage them by telling them how thankful we are to God for them and how we have asked his blessing to be on them.

Questions for Further Discussion

1. What gives you joy in prayer? Do our prayers become less joyful when we pray for those in need? What can we do to rejoice more in prayer?

2. Do you often thank God for the faith of other Christians? Do you thank him for hope? How can we focus more in prayer on what God has done for us spiritually?

3. What is holiness? How does God make us holy? What part does prayer play?

4. How often have you resolved to do something good and then neglected to do it? How often have you heard prayers that God would strengthen our resolve?

5. What keeps us from sharing our faith with others? What should we pray concerning this?

Try This Week

As you pray for those who are sick, also take a moment to pray for their spiritual health, that God might increase their holiness.

A Book to Read

For more on holiness and prayer, see J. I. Packer, *Rediscovering Holiness: Know the Fullness of Life with God* (Ventura, CA: Regal, 2009).

Chapter 20

"GIVE THANKS IN ALL CIRCUMSTANCES"
Prayer as Gratitude

"Rejoice always, pray without ceasing, give thanks in all circumstances; for this is the will of God in Christ Jesus for you."

1 THESSALONIANS 5:16-18

As we have seen, Paul is a man of prayer. He prays for the churches but he also gives them instructions on how to pray. Like most Christians today, his readers probably associated the word "prayer" with making a request from God. Asking God for what we need is part of prayer, but it does not exhaust its meaning.

Giving Thanks
(2 Corinthians 8:16; Ephesians 5:19-20; Colossians 3:15-17; I Thessalonians 5:16-18; I Timothy 1:12-14)

Paul frequently reminds his readers that thanksgiving is also a necessary part of prayer. Praising and thanking God for his marvelous gifts is prayer's true essence. Paul models this spirit of thanksgiving by breaking out in prayer in the middle of his letters. For example, in the middle of a discussion of the contribution for the Christians in Judea he says, "But thanks be to God who put in the heart of Titus the same eagerness for you that I myself had." (2 Corinthians 8:16). Titus' concern for the

Corinthians did not spring from himself; it was the gift of God. To Paul any attitude that promoted the spread of the gospel and led to unity among Christians was a gift of God. Today we need the same faith to see spiritual growth in the church as a gift of God. Like Paul, we should be thankful for that gift.

At times our hearts are so full of the joy of thanksgiving that we cannot express it in mere words. At those times, only song can truly express our gratitude:

> And let the peace of Christ rule in your hearts, to which indeed you were called in one body. And be thankful. Let the word of Christ dwell in you richly; teach and admonish one another in all wisdom; and with gratitude in your hearts sing psalms, hymns, and spiritual songs to God. And whatever you do, in word or deed, do everything in the name of the Lord Jesus, giving thanks to God the Father through him. (Colossians 3:15-17; see also Ephesians 5:18-20)

Singing does many things for the Christian. Christ's word dwells within us as we sing. We teach and encourage one another in song. Most importantly, we praise our holy God in song, singing with gratitude in our hearts for all he has done for us. These songs of thanksgiving are also prayers to him.

But what if we don't feel like singing? What if we've had a terrible day? What if we can't find anything to be thankful for? The Bible says sing anyway. Pray even when you don't feel like it. Be thankful even in trouble. As Paul says, ". . . giving thanks to God the Father at all times and for everything in the name of our Lord Jesus Christ" (Ephesians 5:20).

How can we be thankful at *all* times? How can we sing with gratitude when we don't feel it? Is Paul demanding the impossible or is he advocating hypocrisy? Does he want us to fake our gratitude when we are not in the mood to be genuinely grateful?

None of the above. Paul simply realized that thankfulness is not an emotion but an attitude. Paul himself did not always feel like thanking God. Stoned, shipwrecked, beaten, imprisoned, and even given a thorn in the flesh, he knew the meaning of suffering and pain, yet he could give thanks at all times and for all things. How? Because he trusted God to bring good out of evil, blessing out of suffering. He knew his current pains could not be compared with the glory he would receive. That's how he and Silas could sing praises from a prison cell (Acts 16:25).

So are we to thank God for the trouble that comes upon us? Can we honestly thank God for broken bones, for terminal diseases, for the loss of our loved ones? No. Our loving Father does not send evil. Paul's thorn in the flesh was from Satan, not from God (2 Corinthians 12:9). God did not remove the thorn, but he used that evil as an occasion to give grace: "My grace is sufficient for you" (2 Corinthians 12:9). We are not thankful for trouble, but we can thank God for everything that happens to us if we trust him to suffer with us and to turn our pain to glory. And that is precisely what he has promised.

Thus Paul can say: "Rejoice always, pray without ceasing, give thanks in all circumstances; for this is the will of God in Christ Jesus for you" (1 Thessalonians 5:16-18). God's will is for us to give thanks in all circumstances. No matter what horrors face us in life, there is always something to be thankful for, so we can pray without ceasing. When suffering, don't stop praying, but find some way to be thankful to God.

Our salvation is one thing we can always thank God for. When trouble comes we know God still loves us because he sent his Son to save us:

> I am grateful to Jesus Christ our Lord, who has strengthened me, because he judged me faithful and appointed me to his service, even though I was formerly a blasphemer, a persecutor, and a man of violence. But I received mercy because I had acted ignorantly in unbelief, and the grace of our Lord overflowed for me with the faith and love that are in Christ Jesus. The saying is sure and worthy of full acceptance, that Jesus Christ came into the world to save sinners—of whom I am foremost. (1 Timothy 1:12-15)

Paul can stand any hardship because God saved him, the foremost of sinners, saved him when he was on the road to Damascus to kill more Christians. Paul never forgot he was a sinner, but neither did he forget the grace of God. So he could be grateful to God no matter what came his way.

Today trouble comes to us and threatens to overwhelm. We cry in pain wondering how a loving God could allow this to happen to his children, but we should not doubt his love. If he did not spare his own Son for us, will he not give us all we need? Surely he will. And for that we are always thankful.

Public Prayer
(1 Corinthians 11:2-16; 14:13-19; 1 Timothy 2:1-8)

There are times for us to pray alone, times for us to pray with a few fellow Christians, but also times when the whole church prays together. These public prayers take place as we worship each Sunday and at other times when churches assemble. Christian assemblies in the first century were quite different from ours in some ways, but they always included corporate prayer to God. The Corinthian church had severe problems in their worship—drunkenness at the Lord's Supper, divisions in the assembly, confusion when several spoke in tongues or prophesied at once—so Paul writes them concerning propriety in worship and public prayer:

> Any man who prays or prophesies with something on his head disgraces his head, but any woman who prays or prophesies with her head unveiled disgraces her head—it is one and the same thing as having her head shaved.
>
> Judge for yourselves: is it proper for a woman to pray to God with her head unveiled? Does not nature itself teach you that if a man wears long hair, it is degrading to him, but if a woman has long hair, it is her glory? For her hair is given to her for a covering. But if anyone is disposed to be contentious—we have no such custom, nor do the churches of God. (1 Corinthians 11:4-5, 13-16)

In this lengthy passage, Paul speaks of a custom familiar to his readers but foreign to our society: the wearing of veils. He also speaks to a hot topic in the contemporary church: the role of women in worship and church leadership. These are interesting and important topics, but our question is what this passage has to say to the church concerning prayer.

Avoiding Paul's difficult arguments on veils, authority, and angels, one teaching on public prayer clearly comes through. He assumes both men and women will pray when the church comes together. Does this mean women lead prayer? I'm not sure. "Leading in prayer" is a relatively recent church practice. In Corinth, it appears that different individuals as moved by the Holy Spirit would pray out loud in the assembly. Thus a man or a woman might pray aloud. Paul is not attempting to keep women from praying, but does want to make sure both women and men wear acceptable cultural dress as they pray.

Women as well as men need to pray in church. Of course, when someone leads in prayer, all Christians in the assembly, whether male or female, pray with the leader. Paul may be saying more than that. There are times when several Christians should raise their voices to God in prayer, one at a time, and some of those voices might be feminine. Our churches might be stronger if we heard more of our brothers and sisters pray aloud. This does not mean all distinctions between men and women disappear in church, for the primary purpose of this passage is to dispel that notion. But women, no less than men, are heirs of salvation and have a Father who hears their prayers.

Paul's second concern with public prayer in Corinth is that it be understandable. Several Corinthians could speak in tongues or pray in a special language. Such prayer was helpful in private, but in public assemblies of the church it did not build up other Christians and confused the outsider:

> For if I pray in a tongue, my spirit prays but my mind is unproductive. What should I do then? I will pray with the spirit, but I will pray with the mind also; I will sing praise with the spirit, but I will sing praise with the mind also. Otherwise, if you say a blessing with the spirit, how can anyone in the position of an outsider say the "Amen" to your thanksgiving, since the outsider does not know what you are saying? For you may give thanks well enough, but the other person is not built up. I thank God that I speak in tongues more than all of you; nevertheless, in church I would rather speak five words with my mind, in order to instruct others also, than ten thousand words in a tongue. (1 Corinthians 14:14-19)

Tongue speaking is another controversial topic among contemporary Christians. Some claim to speak in tongues, others dispute that claim. This passage clearly says that even if one can speak in tongues, there is no place for the gift in public prayer. Prayer with other Christians must be understood. All must be able to say "Amen" to the prayer.

But what if we cannot speak in tongues or do not even believe the gift is available today? Does this passage have a message for the non-charismatic? Yes. The principle that public prayer must be understood applies to all churches. Tongues are not the only obstacle to understanding prayer. Mumbling, using an unfamiliar vocabulary, slipping into a strange "prayer tone," and praying only for our personal situation can all make for obscure public prayers. We should be clear when we pray in church, for all are praying with us. We should even consider the outsiders who come to our assembly. Our worship should not confuse or offend them. If they are offended, it must be by the offense of the gospel not by our confusing prayers.

Public prayer should be focused in two directions at once: to God, who is the only one to whom we speak in prayer; and to our fellow Christians, for we pray to God together. Public prayer speaks only to God, but it should also build up our brothers and sisters.

What kind of prayers should be offered in public? For whom should we pray? How should we pray? Paul tackles these questions in 1 Timothy:

> First of all, then, I urge that supplications, prayers, intercessions, and thanks-givings be made for everyone, for kings and all who are in high positions so that we may lead a quiet and peaceable life in all godliness and dignity.
>
> I desire, then, that in every place the men should pray, lifting up holy hands without anger or argument.... (1 Timothy 2:1-2, 8)

Four words are used here to describe prayer. "Supplications" are heartfelt requests to God for help through personal difficulty. "Prayers" also implies requests from God, but in a broader sense of asking for his care in all circumstances. "Intercessions" are prayers for those around us: we petition God on behalf of our brothers, sisters, and neighbors. "Thanksgivings" spring naturally from our gratitude for God's gifts. These terms do not so much describe four separate types of prayer, but point to elements found in most public prayers. In church we make requests to God for ourselves and for others and we thank him for his blessings.

We pray these prayers for everyone, but particularly for kings and those in high position. In Paul's day many rulers persecuted Christians, yet they are told to pray even for unjust rulers in hope that God will make the bad kings leave Christians in peace. No matter what kind of government rules us, we still pray that the authorities will allow us to live quiet and peaceable lives.

As far as how to pray, we are told to lift up holy hands. This raises the question of bodily posture in prayer. The Bible gives many positions for prayer: standing, kneeling, bowing the face to the ground, lifting hands, and others. No one position is promoted as the only proper way of praying. In public or private prayer we may kneel or bow or stand or raise hands. What we may not do is belittle a brother or sister who prays in a different position. Prayer must be without anger or argument. Neither should we adopt an unusual prayer position to call attention to ourselves and our hyper-spirituality. Our church's custom should dictate our practice. Public prayer is a time for Christians to be united in their petitions to God. It is not a time (indeed, there is never an acceptable time) for us to bicker and argue over how we pray. Attitude, not posture, determines the genuineness of our prayers.

Having said this, it does appear to me that our posture says something about our attitude in prayer. In the Old Testament, it was common to throw oneself face downward in prayer to express respect for the Almighty. In my own boyhood I remember how sincerely impressed I was to see men and women kneeling in prayer. Too much can be made of "body language," but I can't help but wonder why we stopped kneeling: was it the inconvenience or a lack of reverence?

Whatever our posture, something special happens when the church prays together. The routine of our worship services may blind us to the beauty of corporate prayer. In a world where everyone looks out for number one, Christians put aside their differences and join together to approach their Father and encourage each other. What could be more beautiful?

Questions for Further Discussion

1. Does something special happen when we sing prayers? What are some of your favorite prayer hymns? Why do sung prayers sometimes seem more meaningful than spoken prayers?

2. Did women pray with men in Corinth? Do you think the women prayed out loud? Does this happen today? Should it?

3. What are some ways we pray together without only one person leading? Should we pray more often in these ways?

4. Discuss the difference between supplications, prayers, intercession, and thanksgiving. Should all our prayers include these?

5. Does posture in prayer make a difference? Why do we fail to use some biblical postures?

Try This Week

When you pray alone this week, try lifting your hands in praise and thanksgiving. At the end of the week reflect on how this affected your experience of prayer.

A Book to Read

For an interesting book on prayer postures, see Doug Pagitt and Kathryn Prill, *BodyPrayer: The Posture of Intimacy with God* (Colorado Springs: WaterBrook, 2005).

Chapter 21

"Pray in the Spirit at All Times"
Prayer as Spiritual Communion

"Pray in the Spirit at all times."

Ephesians 6:18

In his letters Paul gives thanks for the churches and prays God will grant them certain spiritual blessings. He does not, however, think himself spiritually superior to his readers; he not only prays for them, he requests their prayers.

Requesting Prayer
(Romans 15:30-33; 2 Corinthians 1:8-11; Philippians 1:19; Ephesians 6:18-20; Colossians 4:2-4; I Thessalonians 5:25; 2 Thessalonians 3:1-5)

Paul is not a spiritual loner. He knows his limitations and knows there are many who oppose the gospel. Thus, he frequently asks his fellow Christians to support him through prayer:

> I appeal to you, brothers and sisters, by our Lord Jesus Christ and by the love of the Spirit, to join me in earnest prayer to God on my behalf, that I may be rescued from the unbelievers in Judea, and that my ministry to Jerusalem may be acceptable to the saints, so that by God's will I may come to you with joy and be refreshed in your company. The God of peace be with all of you. Amen. (Romans 15:30-33)

Two nagging concerns overshadowed Paul's coming trip to Jerusalem. One was the opposition he would face there. This was no figment of Paul's imagination: already the unbelieving Jews had tried to kill him (Acts 9:29-30). Their hatred of Paul was understandable. To them he was a turncoat, one who had stood firm for the Law and against these wayward Jews who were loyal to the Nazarene, but had himself been deceived into following Jesus. Paul knew their hatred and their power, so he asks the Romans to pray for his deliverance that he might afterward come to visit them in Rome (Romans 15:32; see also Philemon 1:22). Their prayer for Paul is answered, though not in the way Paul expected. He is indeed delivered from death in Jerusalem, but he comes to Rome in chains, a prisoner of the unbelievers (Acts 21:27-28:31).

This is not the only time that Paul faced danger from unbelievers. Everywhere he went, he made enemies. In Asia, he faced a severe trial that threatened to completely crush his spirit (2 Corinthians 1:8-11). But God rescued him and he is confident God will save him again. Paul has this confidence through prayer. He asks the Corinthians as well as the Romans to "join us by helping us by your prayers" (2 Corinthians 1:11; see also Philippians 1:19; 2 Thessalonians 3:1-2). Paul never faced opposition alone; through prayer his fellow Christians and his heavenly Father stood beside him.

Paul's second concern regarding his Judean trip seems less realistic: he worries that his ministry to the Jerusalem church (the gift of money he has collected from the Gentile churches) will not be accepted. Why would the Jerusalem Christian reject a gift for the poor, a gift they themselves had asked Paul to remember (see Acts 11:27-30; Galatians 2:10)? Because this was no ordinary gift. It was a gift from predominantly Gentile churches to the Jewish church in Jerusalem. Paul intended for this gift to cement relations between Jews and Gentiles in the church since it demonstrated the love of Gentile Christians for their Jewish brothers and sisters. By receiving the gift, the Jerusalem church would be admitting that Gentiles are fully heirs of Christ along with the Jews.

Don't forget that the Judaizers dogged Paul's every step. They refused to admit Gentiles into the church unless they first became Jews. These Judaizers were influential in the Jerusalem church and it would not be out of character for them to let people starve rather than compromising their principles to receive a gift from Gentiles. Paul then is requesting the Romans to pray for unity among Christians. Their prayer was answered: the Jerusalem church accepted Paul warmly (Acts 21:17-20).

What do these requests for prayer say to Christians today? We also face opposition from unbelievers. They may not try to kill us, but they can insult and wound. God will deliver us from such people if we pray. We also face disunity and bad feelings between Christians. We can join to pray for unity, so that the good gifts we have for one another will be warmly accepted.

When we are ridiculed for our Christian faith, our first reaction is to keep a low profile, to soft-peddle our Christianity, or to keep completely quiet about it. Paul faced more than ridicule; he faced imprisonment, beatings, and death. He would have been less than human if he were not at times tempted to be quiet about Christ. Facing that temptation, he asks the churches to pray for him:

> Pray also for me, so that when I speak, a message may be given to me to make known with boldness the mystery of the gospel, for which I am an ambassador in chains. Pray that I might declare it boldly, as I must speak. (Ephesians 6:19-20)

> Devote yourselves to prayer, keeping alert in it with thanksgiving. At the same time pray for us as well that God will open a door for the word, that we may declare the mystery of Christ, for which I am in prison, so that I may reveal it clearly, as I should. (Colossians 4:2-4)

In these passages Paul asks for boldness to proclaim the mystery of the gospel. He knows opposition can make his witness timid. He knows how easy it is to soften the offensive teachings of the Christian message, so he prays he may reveal Christ clearly.

The puny opposition we face from a hostile culture tempts us also to weaken our witness. We say, "Yes, I'm a Christian, but I don't condemn those who aren't," or "I believe the Bible, but if you don't, you're entitled to your opinion," or "I don't want to force my beliefs on anyone." Or we say nothing at all. We are completely silent about our faith in the presence of unbelievers. But if Jesus was who he said he was, and if we take our faith seriously, then we cannot help but tell the good news. If Christianity is true, it should be "forced" on people, that is, they should be led to admit its truth for their own happiness. What we proclaim is good news. Christian witness is not optional. If we fail to confess him, he will fail to confess us.

But where can we get the courage to confess Christ when it is embarrassing and may even cost us friendships, promotions, and acceptance? Only in prayer. If the bold apostle Paul needed to ask for courage and boldness, surely we need to ask. And we should pray for other Christians to be emboldened by God.

Christians were never meant to live their Christian lives alone. Our prayer lives are not to be merely private. Like Paul we need at times to say, "Beloved, pray for us" (1 Thessalonians 5:25). It is only through the prayers of our brothers and sisters and the blessing of our heavenly Father that we can live the demanding life of a bold Christian.

Prayer, Anxiety, and Suffering
(Romans 12:12; 2 Corinthians 12:7-10; Philippians 4:6-7)

As Christians we need a consistent prayer life in all circumstances. But there are times when prayer is particularly called for. Jesus prayed in the crises of his life. The early Christians prayed at the turning points in the life of the church. We too should pray in the face of suffering and anxiety.

Paul tells the Romans, "Rejoice in hope, be patient in suffering, persevere in prayer" (Romans 12:12). The pressures of life sometimes threaten to overwhelm us. In our despair we may be tempted to stop praying, thinking, "What's the use?" But perseverance in prayer leads to patience in suffering, and no matter how bad things get, we can still rejoice in the hope of resurrection. Our suffering may even be fatal, but it is not final. God holds us in his hand.

These two strange bedfellows—rejoicing and suffering—are found together in other New Testament passages. Paul urges the Philippians to rejoice and be thankful even in the midst of anxiety: "Rejoice in the Lord always; again I will say, Rejoice. Let your gentleness be known to everyone. The Lord is near. Do not worry about anything, but in everything by prayer and supplication with thanksgiving let your requests be made known to God. And the peace of God, which passes all understanding, will guard your hearts and your minds in Christ Jesus" (Philippians 4:4-7). This is one of the most reassuring Scriptures in the Bible. Christian joy stems not from circumstances, but from the realization that "The Lord is near." The lives we lead produce great anxiety, but if we thankfully take that worry to God, he will give us peace that passes understanding.

The sure solution to worry promised by these verses is quite different from the prescriptions of our age. Paul does not urge us to think positively, to believe in ourselves, or to minimize the reasons for our worry. Dedicated Christians have good reason to be worried; after all, the world is against us. The peace we are promised is not the result of a twelve-step program or any particular technique (as helpful as they may be). It is the free gift of God in prayer. It is a peace that passes understanding because it is not based on the pleasantness of our circumstances, but on our trust in a Father who guards us.

It is also a strange peace because even when we persist in prayer, God does not always relieve the cause of our anxiety. Paul knew this personally. When he speaks of pain and anxiety, he speaks not as a bystander, but as one who knew them intimately:

> Therefore to keep me from being too elated, a thorn was given me in the flesh, a messenger of Satan to torment me, to keep me from being too elated. Three times I appealed to the Lord about this, that it would leave me, but he said to me, "My grace is sufficient for you, for power is made perfect in weakness." So, I will boast all the more gladly of my weaknesses, so that the power of Christ may dwell in me. Therefore I am content with weaknesses, insults, hardships, persecutions, and calamities for the sake of Christ; for whenever I am weak, then I am strong. (2 Corinthians 12:7-10)

Speculation on the exact nature of Paul's thorn in the flesh is fruitless; whatever it may have been, it caused him pain and anxiety. He does not blame God for the thorn, it is "a messenger of Satan," but he does make his request for relief to God. God's answer: "My grace is sufficient for you."

What kind of answer is this? Did God not promise to heal our hurts and remove our worries? Yes. And that is precisely what he does for Paul. He does not remove the pain, but he makes it of no account; he places it in a new perspective. "My grace is enough," God says, "for my power is made perfect in weakness." God did not send the thorn, but he is so powerful he can take this evil thing and use it for Paul's good. Paul is not healed, but his anxiety is taken away as his pain is swallowed up in the grace of God.

God's answer to Paul and the three prayers Paul offers reminds us of another sufferer who cried to God in pain. Like Jesus in Gethsemane, Paul has a cross to bear. Like Jesus, he trusts the will of the Father.

Jesus and Paul are not alone. Each Christian takes up the cross. We are called to suffer with Jesus. God promises us relief from pain and anxiety, but he does not promise our sicknesses will always be cured or our path always be made smooth. In pain we cry to God, and he hears us. He may remove the pain, or he may say, "My grace is enough, you must bear this cross." That answer should be enough for us, for he suffers with us, perfecting us in weakness and giving us a sure hope.

The Help of the Spirit
(Romans 8:26-28; Ephesians 6:18)

All this sounds marvelous, but can we really do it? Can we really pray that God's will be done? Can we be happy with God's answer if he chooses not to heal our pain? What should we pray for? Healing? Faith? Courage? Resignation? How do we know what God's will is for us?

All of these questions point to one fact: when it comes to prayer, we need help. The good news is: we have it. "Likewise the Spirit helps us in our weakness; for we do not know how to pray as we ought, but that very Spirit intercedes with sighs too deep for words. And God, who searches the heart, knows what is the mind of the Spirit, because the Spirit intercedes for the saints according to the will of God." (Romans 8:26-27)

"We do not know how to pray as we ought." Truer words were never spoken. Like the disciples, we ask, "Lord, teach us to pray." But this passage deals less with the technique of prayer than with the content of prayer. Not only do we not know the right words to say, we do not even know what to pray for. We all have had loved ones on the verge of death. For what should we pray? For healing? Perhaps, for even if the doctors have given up hope, our God still has life in his hands. But what if it is not God's will to heal them? Do we pray they face death with courage? Do we pray for a quick and painless death?

These are not hypothetical questions. We all have struggled with these situations. But we do not pray alone; the Spirit prays with us. The Spirit takes our stumbling words, our doubts, and our struggles and translates them into "sighs too deep for words." We don't always know how to speak to God, but the Spirit knows, and he speaks for us. The effectiveness of prayer depends not on our ability to speak or on the clarity of our desires, but on the power of the Spirit.

Praying in the Spirit is the rule, not the exception of the Christian's prayer life. Truly spiritual prayer is not measured by how we feel or how right we get the words. We don't have to pray "good" to pray in the Spirit. Even when we have no idea what to pray, even when we don't want to pray, the Spirit is there to help us. Yes, particularly when we just can't seem to pray, the Spirit intercedes. He amplifies our groanings as God's own megaphone. And God hears our cry.

So what should keep us from praying? Trouble? No, we are to take our worries to God. Our sins? No, for we rely on God's grace in prayer. Our own ineptitude? No, for the Spirit speaks for us. If we "pray in the Spirit at all times" (Ephesians 6:18), then our prayers are always adequate, even when we are not. We have no excuse, not even ourselves, for neglecting to pray.

Questions for Further Discussion

1. Are you ever in danger from unbelievers? Do we need to pray for boldness to speak God's word? What keeps us from speaking it?

2. Does prayer solve worry? How? Why don't we pray more and worry less?

3. Like Paul, have you ever prayed hard to have a problem removed and God did not remove it? Did that make you less likely to pray? Should it?

4. How does the Spirit help us when we pray? Do you think about and ask for the Spirit's help?

5. What keeps us from praying more?

Try This Week

In your prayers, claim the promise of the help of the Spirit.

A Book to Read

Paul's view of the Spirit is unfolded in Gordon Fee, *Paul, the Spirit, and the People of God* (Peabody, MA: Hendrickson, 1996).

Chapter 22

"Ask in Faith, Never Doubting"
Prayer as Confidence

"But ask in faith, never doubting."

JAMES 1:6

The Gospels, Acts, and Paul are not the only New Testament books to mention prayer. Indeed, almost every New Testament book discusses prayer, showing how central prayer is to the life of the disciples.

Prayer in Hebrews
(Hebrews 5:7-10; 7:23-25; 13:18-19)

Hebrews is an unusual book. We are not sure who wrote it or who originally received it. It does not read like a letter or a history or a Gospel. Most scholars now believe Hebrews is a written sermon, since the author himself calls it a "brief word of exhortation" (Hebrews 13:22). To contemporary Christians it must seem like a strange sermon. It is not brief, at least not by our standards. It contains detailed arguments and obscure terminology from Old Testament sacrificial passages that contemporary audiences find difficult, if not downright impossible to follow.

In spite of its strangeness to the contemporary mind, Hebrews is a book to be treasured by contemporary Christians. The writer of Hebrews displays the superiority and finality of Jesus and he urges his readers to be faithful to the pioneer of their salvation. In his reflection on the superiority of Jesus' high priesthood, he harks back to the prayers in Gethsemane: "In the days of his flesh, Jesus offered up prayers and supplications, with loud cries and tears, to the one who was able to save him from death, and he was heard because of his reverent submission"(Hebrews 5:7). In the garden, with loud cries and tears, Jesus begged the Father to save him from death, yet he prayed, "Your will be done."

When we read the Gospel accounts of Jesus in Gethsemane, it may seem God did not hear Jesus' prayer; after all, Jesus did not receive what he asked for. He still had to go to the cross. According to Hebrews, God heard Jesus' prayer in the garden. In what sense did God hear his prayer? Does this simply mean God heard him but said no to his request? I don't think so. To have ones prayer heard means to be answered, to receive God's blessing. The Hebrew writer contends God answered Jesus' prayer to be saved from death, but he did not answer in the way Jesus intended in his prayer. Christ still had to drink the cup to go to the cross, but the Father saved him from death by raising him from the dead.

Perhaps, like me, you've heard that God answers prayer one of three ways: Yes, No and Not Yet. This passage from Hebrews makes it clear that God has only one answer. If we ask in faith, and ask in the will of God as Jesus did in the garden, then God always answers, "Yes." That "yes" however, may take a form beyond our wildest dreams: resurrection, new life, new self.

There is an important lesson here for us. God does not always give us what we want or think we need, but he always hears us and gives us something better than what we request. We may ask for relief from pain, for comfort for our broken hearts, for ease for our tired souls. He may not give us these. His answer may be, "My grace is sufficient for you," or "You must bear your cross," but he has a greater gift for us: the gift of resurrection, of new life. When we pray as Christians, we pray not with a shallow optimism that things will immediately get better, but we pray with a sure hope that God will hear and bless in his own way and time. Like Jesus in the garden, we may have to learn obedience through suffering (Hebrews 5:8-10), but like him we must maintain our faith in a loving Father who holds life in his hand and who answers our prayers.

By learning obedience, Jesus became our great high priest, the one who takes our sins to the Father:

Furthermore, the former priests were many in number, because they were prevented by death from continuing in office; but he holds his priesthood permanently, because he continues forever. Consequently he is able for all time to save those who approach God through him, since he always lives to make intercession for them. (Hebrews 7:23-25)

Jesus is our priest forever; he saves us for all time. Old Testament priests offered sacrifices to cover the people's sins. Jesus offered himself for us once for all (Hebrews 7:27). As both our sacrifice and our priest, he lives to make intercession for us.

Why do we need intercession? Don't we have a heavenly Father who loves us and listens to us? Yes, but our sins have torn us away from the Father, blocking our path to the Most Holy God. But our Savior intercedes for us in prayer. He removes our sin, makes us right with God, and makes our requests for us. We can approach God boldly, for when we pray Christ our priest and sacrifice prays with us. Our prayers become his prayers to the Father. He lives to pray for us.

The other reference to prayer in Hebrews sounds quite familiar: "Pray for us; we are sure that we have a clear conscience, desiring to act honorably in all things. I urge you all the more to do this, so that I may be restored to you very soon" (Hebrews 13:18-19).

As we saw with Paul, no Christian is so mature that he can afford to do without the prayers of fellow Christians. The Hebrew writer, like Paul, asks his readers to pray that he may see them soon, that he might "be restored to you." This is an intriguing phrase. Has there been bad blood between the writer and his readers? Is that why he insists he has a clear conscience? What has prevented him from going to them? Imprisonment? Sickness? Their own attitude? His work in other ministries? We are not told, but we do know he now wants to see them and he asks them to pray that he will.

Nothing should separate Christian brothers and sisters. Too many times we allow things to come between us and fellow Christians. Perhaps an inappropriate word was said, perhaps we felt ignored or ridiculed, perhaps we simply grew distant from neglect. From Hebrews we learn that the barriers existing between Christians can be torn away by prayer.

Prayer in James

James is full of practical advice for Christians and so we would expect him to teach on prayer. At the very beginning of his book, after urging his readers to find joy even in trials, he tells them to ask for wisdom:

> If any of you is lacking in wisdom, ask God, who gives to all generously and ungrudgingly, and it will be given you. But ask in faith, never doubting, for the one who doubts is like a wave of the sea, driven and tossed by the wind; for the doubter, being double-minded and unstable in every way, must not expect to receive anything from the Lord. (James 1:5-8)

Although the word "prayer" does not occur in this passage, we discover much of importance on how to ask God for what we need. We are told to ask for wisdom, something we need and God wants to give us. We especially need wisdom to see our daily trials as opportunities to strengthen our faith. We can pray in confidence knowing the God to whom we pray is generous and will give us the wisdom we need.

Yet this is no automatic transaction. James warns us to be careful how we ask. Our petitions to God must not be half-hearted; we cannot be in two minds as to whether God will bless. God is good. God is great. He will give us what we need. All that prevents him from doing so are our own doubts. James is not questioning God's power to give, but rather our power to receive. How in the world can we expect to get wisdom from God, if we are foolish enough to doubt him? James echoes the words of Jesus, ". . . have faith and do not doubt" (Matthew 21:21).

Doubt is not the only hindrance to prayer. Conflict, apathy, and selfishness also block our way to God:

> Those conflicts and disputes among you, where do they come from? Do they not come from your cravings that are at war within you? You want something and do not have it; so you commit murder. And you covet something and cannot obtain it; so you engage in disputes and conflicts. You do not have because you do not ask. You ask and do not receive, because you ask wrongly, in order to spend what you get on your pleasures. (James 4:1-3)

Why is it we do not get what we want from God? One reason, James says, is we do not ask. Why don't we always ask God for what we want? We may realize what we want is not what we truly need. Or perhaps we doubt God's power or desire to help us. Maybe we think we can get what we want without his help; self-sufficiency gets in the way of prayer. Or it all could be due to lack of effort on our part; we simply do not take the time to ask. It is not as though God needs us to ask before he can bless, he already knows what we need, but for our own sake, we need to ask.

Will God give us everything we ask for? No. Not if we ask selfishly for what brings pleasure only to us. God is not a genie in a bottle who grants our wishes. Prayer is not a magical formula for wealth or pleasure. When we pray we ask for what is ultimately good and pleasurable, not for immediate gratification of our desires; and we pray with the needs and wants of others in mind, not just for what is best for us.

God will give us wisdom and everything else we need, but not necessarily everything we want. He always answers our prayers, but we must sometimes wait for his answer. However, the need for trust and patience does not mean prayer does not work. James assures us that prayer is powerful:

> Are any among you suffering? They should pray. Are any cheerful? They should sing songs of praise. Are any among you sick? They should call for the elders of the church and have them pray over them, anointing them with oil in the name of the Lord. The prayer of faith will save the sick, and the Lord will raise them up; and anyone who has committed sins will be forgiven. Therefore confess your sins to one another, and pray for one another, so that you may be healed. The prayer of the righteous is powerful and effective. Elijah was a human being like us, and he prayed fervently that it might not rain, and for three years and six months it did not rain on the earth. Then he prayed again, and the heavens gave rain and the earth yielded its harvest. (James 5:13-18)

James lists all the marvelous things God will do for us if we pray for ourselves and for others: he will end our suffering, heal our sickness, and forgive our sins. Prayer to God is beyond a doubt "powerful and effective." Elijah prayed for drought and then for rain as a sign to the Israelites (1 Kings 17:1, 18:1) and God answered his prayers immediately because they were in accordance with his will. We pray with the same fervor and assurance, knowing our prayers are effective if we pray in God's will.

Questions for Further Discussion _____

1. Like Jesus, have you ever prayed with loud cries and tears? Did God answer? Does God answer "yes" to every prayer?

2. Can we pray without doubting? Are we always sure God will give us what we ask? Should we be?

3. Why don't we always ask God for what we want?

4. What prayers are selfish? If we ask for something we want, is that a selfish prayer?

5. Was Elijah really a human being like us? Do we sometimes put biblical characters on too high of a pedestal? How can we avoid that?

Try This Week

Think of something (like wisdom) that you know God wants to give you. This week, pray in complete faith that you will receive it.

A Book to Read

Anthony DeStefano lists prayers we can pray with confidence in *Ten Prayers God Always Says Yes to: Divine Answers to Life's Most Difficult Problems* (New York: Doubleday, 2007).

Chapter 23

"DISCIPLINE YOURSELF FOR THE SAKE OF YOUR PRAYERS"
Prayer as Anticipation

"The end of all things is near; therefore be serious
and discipline yourselves for the sake of your prayers."

1 PETER 4:7

Even the neglected books of the New Testament, the shorter epistles and Revelation, have significant teachings on prayer. These books explore the place of prayer in the life of disciples, clearly displaying its power and beauty.

Prayer in 1 Peter
(1 Peter 3:7; 4:7)

Peter writes "the exiles of the Dispersion" to encourage them to be faithful even though they must suffer as Jesus did. "Exiles" is a significant term; it implies these Christians have been torn from the prevailing social structure because of their faith in Christ. Now they are citizens of a new holy kingdom and their old companions, surprised at their new behavior, ostracize and even persecute them.

This situation was one for prayer. Peter speaks of prayer in this letter in somewhat surprising contexts. Instructing his readers on Christian marriage, he tells wives to accept the authority of their husbands and tells husbands to show consideration for their wives. Following this instruction would, no doubt, promote harmony in the home and set a good example for those outside the church, but these are not the purposes Peter gives for his advice. Instead, wives and husbands are to act this way "so that nothing may hinder your prayers." (I Peter 3:7).

This is the only reference in the New Testament to prayer in marriage (except, perhaps, for 1 Corinthians 7:5), but its off-handed tone implies shared prayer between spouses was taken for granted by early Christians. Trouble between Christian marriage partners is especially disturbing because it gets in the way of their prayers. In our world, not sleeping together is the sure sign of marital difficulty. To Peter, to not be able to pray together is even more devastating to the relationship.

But how often do we pray with those who are dearest to us, our husband, our wife, our children? Are we too busy? Do we consider prayer purely a private affair, none of our family's business? Peter will not allow that. He expects his readers to pray together. If we take the Bible seriously, we must make prayer an integral and central part of our married life.

Peter places prayer in the context of marriage, but also in the context of the end of the world: "The end of all things is near; therefore be serious and discipline yourselves for the sake of your prayers" (1 Peter 4:7). Christians live in the shadow of the cross and in anticipation of the return of Christ. Most Christians today seem to think little about the end of the world. Even when they do, it usually is in terms of idle speculation about the signs of the times. We do not know when he will return, but we are to believe he will. Each generation of Christians lives in the last days. Each can say, "Jesus is coming soon."

If we are convinced his coming is near, our prayer life is changed. Our prayer life becomes something serious, something that should not be played at, but that should be nurtured in a systematic way. Peter's word is "discipline." Discipline is almost a bad word today. We live in the age of freedom, of excess, of feeling good about ourselves. Discipline conjures up images of monks in their cells, or Marines on Paris Island, or the worst of reform schools. The only place one seems to meet discipline today is in the gym. Many are almost religious about their workouts. "No pain, no gain," they say.

Peter's words remind us there is something more important than the health and strength of our bodies, more important than anything in this world. The end of all things is near. Soon all that will be left is the reality of the God to whom we pray. With that in mind, we would do well to pay more attention to our spiritual discipline than our physical workouts. Discipline in prayer means praying regularly, even when we don't feel like it, praying when it is not convenient, even praying when it hurts. Wrestling with God in prayer can be painful, but as with all discipline, "No pain, no gain." The realization that the end of all things is near motivates us to disciplined prayer.

Prayer in John's Epistles

John repeats a theme found throughout the New Testament: ask and you will receive. For the Christian who is clothed with the righteousness of Christ, there is an assurance that God answers prayer: "Beloved, if our hearts do not condemn us, we have boldness before God; and we receive from him whatever we ask, because we obey his commandments and do what pleases him"(1 John 3:21-22).

John's words are similar to the words of Jesus ("Whatever you ask for in prayer in faith, you will receive" Matthew 21:22), and to the advice of James ("But ask in faith, never doubting . . ." James 1:6). To John, however, the confidence that we will receive what we ask from God is based not on faith, but on obedience. John is not advocating a "works righteousness" of demanding perfection from Christians, but he, like James, teaches that faith and obedience are inseparable. True faith leads to obedience, and to obey God is "to believe in the name of his Son Jesus Christ and to love one another" (I John 3:23).

In other words, prayer is part of something much larger; it is Christian prayer only in the context of our entire relationship to God. It is legitimate and right to ask God for what we need, but when we approach him he must not be a stranger to us. We dare not pray only when we are desperate or have exhausted our own resources or when we, quite frankly, have nothing better to do. We pray to our Father and as a loving Father, he gives us what we ask. Such a Father deserves and demands our trust and obedience. It is when "our hearts do not condemn us," when we know our relation to our Father is genuine, that we can approach him boldly.

John not only tells us how to pray ("with boldness"), but also for whom to pray:

And this is the boldness we have in him, that if we ask anything according to his will, he hears us. And if we know that he hears us in whatever we ask, we know we have obtained the requests made of him. If you see your brother or sister committing what is not a mortal sin, you will ask, and God will give life to such a one—to one whose sin is not mortal. There is sin that is mortal; I do not say that you should pray about that. All wrongdoing is sin, but there is a sin that is not mortal. (1 John 5:14-17)

Sin is another little-used word in our society, even in the church. In America we believe strongly in the individual's freedom to do whatever he or she wants, "as long as it doesn't hurt anyone." As part of a church, many Christians feel they should mind their own business, saying Christianity is a purely private affair and the foibles of their fellow Christians are strictly between them and God.

The Bible will not allow us the luxury of a strictly private Christianity. Whether we like it or not, we are responsible for each other. Your sins, even when they are not personally against me, are my business, for you are my brother or sister. Oh yes, my sins are your business too.

This does not make the church a bunch of busybodies, eager to find the latest dirt on others. On the contrary, my concern for your sins should not be to broadcast them or to belittle you, but to hide your sins completely by asking God to forgive them. And when you see me sin, you too are to pray for my forgiveness.

I'm not completely sure what John means about a mortal sin that should not be prayed for; perhaps any sin we refuse to acknowledge can become a mortal sin. But John clearly challenges Christians to honestly confess our sin and take responsibility for our brothers and sisters. Too many times in church we put up a false front. Sure, we admit we are sinners (isn't everyone?), but the last thing we would do is to confess a particular sin.

We are not called to wallow in our sins, to graphically depict our every evil action, but we are expected to confess our sins. What is even more difficult, we are expected to care enough for our fellow Christians to confront them with their sins and pray to God on their behalf. We may not relish those confrontations, but if we are to be God's children, we must pray for our fellow sinners and accept, even welcome their prayers for us.

Praying for fellow Christians is our duty and privilege even when we do not see them sinning. In 3 John, the elder prays for his friend Gaius: "Beloved, I pray that all may go well with you and that you may be in good health, just as it is well with your soul"(3 John 1:2). We pray for other Christians when they sin; we pray for their health; most importantly, we pray for their spiritual health, that it is well with their souls.

Prayer in Revelation

Dragons, beasts with scorpion's tails, plagues on horseback, and jeweled cities: no wonder there is so much interest today in the Book of Revelation. But while many mine it for hidden clues to the time of the Second Coming, they may miss its more obvious teaching on Christian living. For example, in this final book of the New Testament, we have a most beautiful picture of prayer: "Another angel with a golden censer came and stood at the altar; he was given a great quantity of incense to offer with the prayers of all the saints on the golden altar that is before the throne. And the smoke of the incense, with the prayers of the saints, rose before God from the hand of the angel" (Revelation 8:3-4; see also 5:8).

As the Jews in the Old Testament offered incense to God in the Temple, so we worship God in prayer. Our prayers go up to God as pleasing incense. He wants us to pray. He gladly receives the prayers of the saints. It is appropriate that this is the final word of the New Testament on prayer. Prayer is sublime not because it has some inherent power or because we have the ability to pray beautifully. Prayer is sublime because the Lord God almighty desires us to pray, hears our prayers, and generously blesses. It is not the scent of our offerings that counts, but the glory of the one who receives them.

Questions for Further Discussion _____

1. What is the role of prayer in marriage? What can we do to make it more a part of our family life?

2. What are some ways we can discipline ourselves in prayer?

3. What does it mean to pray in light of the Second Coming?

4. What does obedience have to do with prayer? Should we not pray for certain disobedient people?

5. Do you most often pray for the physical or the spiritual health of others?

Try This Week

If married, pray this week with your spouse. If single, pray with a friend.

A Book to Read

For examples of prayers rooted in anticipation of God's redemption, see *Awed to Heaven, Rooted in Earth: Prayers of Walter Brueggemann* (Minneapolis: Augsburg Fortress, 2003).

Conclusion

"Lord Teach Us to Pray"
Following the Dangerous Path of Prayer

What have we learned from this study of prayer in the Bible? Our quick glance at dozens of biblical passages should not lull us into thinking we are now experts on prayer. But although we still have much to learn, the following lessons are clear.

We Pray to a Powerful and Loving Father

The primary fact of prayer is not the act of prayer, but the one to whom we pray. Prayer would be a waste of time if addressed to a Deity who did not love us or who could not deliver what he had promised. But our God has all power. His arm is never too short to reach us. Jesus reminds us of that power when he tells us prayer can move mountains. Paul reminds us of that power when he says God can do more than we ask or think. The early church trusted that power to deliver them against impossible odds.

We live in an age of limits; an age where science determines what is possible. Our God is not bound by limits. He stands outside our age and our universe, holding both in his hands. No task is beyond him. No cause too hopeless. No outlook too bleak. Whatever we ask, God can do.

But an all-powerful God is no good to us if he is too far removed. Our God is our intimate. Our troubles are his. Good news is ours: God is not only power, he is love. He loved us enough to send his Son. He loves us enough to make us his children. He wants only to bless, to give good gifts.

We have no need to trick God to bless us. Magical phrases or eternal repetition cannot manipulate him. If we simply speak to our loving Father in faith, his power will be ours.

We Pray with a Loving Savior

When the disciples asked, "Lord, teach us to pray," Jesus gave them the Lord's Prayer. But that is not the only way he teaches us to pray. In all his prayers he shows us the true path of discipleship. He often prayed alone; so should we. He prayed in the rough spots of life; so should we. He prayed not just for himself, but for others. He prayed the Father's will be done.

But he is more than our example in prayer. He is that, and it is a marvel beyond belief that God not only allows us to pray but he also prays himself in the person of his Son. But Jesus not only models prayer, he not only prays for us, he prays with us. When we pray in his name we pray like him, we pray with his authority, but what is more, he meets us in prayer. By the Spirit our prayers are joined with his. He intercedes for us. He makes our prayers his own. If the loving Father hears us as his children, how much more will he hear his beloved Son as he prays with us?

We Are Helped in Prayer by the Holy Spirit

"We do not pray as we ought," Paul says. Thank God we do not have to pray correctly to be heard. The effectiveness of our prayers does not depend on our own abilities. We have help. We have a helper: the Holy Spirit. He intercedes for us, translating our pitiful attempts at expression into ineffable words that touch the heart of the Father. Whenever we pray sincerely and in faith, we pray in the Spirit.

So the heart of Christian prayer is this: prayer is from beginning to end a work of God. God the Father is the object of prayer, the powerful, loving one to whom we pray. God the Son is our model and companion in prayer; we pray in his name and he prays with us. God the Spirit is our helper in prayer, turning our words into God's words.

This takes the pressure off us in prayer. Yes, we should pray in the right way for the right things. Yes, we must learn to pray. Yes, we should discipline ourselves to pray. But we never pray alone. We have all the help we need.

We Learn to Pray

Prayer is not a natural ability. Most everyone has prayed sometime, but Christian prayer is a learned activity. The disciples knew Jewish prayers, perhaps they were even taught to pray by John the Baptist, but they still felt the need to learn from Jesus.

How do we learn to pray? Through studies like this one. The Bible teaches us to pray. As we see the biblical men and women wrestle with God in prayer, we imitate their faith. As we watch Jesus pray, we learn to pray.

How do we learn to pray? Through the examples of our fellow Christians. We learn to pray from our mothers and fathers. We learn prayer in church, watching the spiritual giants around us. We pray with them and before too long we find ourselves praying like them.

How do we learn to pray? Practice, practice, practice. One learns to pray by praying. By praying regularly, even when our feelings are mixed and our thoughts confused, we build up our praying strength by praying. Prayer teaches prayer.

We Should Pray Alone

At times it is easy to pray: when someone leads a prayer at a meal, at prayer time in church, when someone says, "Let's pray together." What is difficult is blocking out time for private prayer. Even Jesus had trouble finding time to pray alone. The crowds doggedly hunted for him. To find the time, he awoke early in the morning and stole away from his disciples, or he stayed awake all night in prayer.

These or other ingenious schemes could help us make time for private prayer. The greatest obstacle to our prayers is ourselves. It takes a burning desire to pray to move one to lose sleep. There will always be plenty of reasons or excuses for not praying. Just do it. Pray. We are promised if we do speak to God in our secret room he will hear and reward us openly.

We Should Pray with Other Christians

Small group prayer is a special blessing from God. When one or more Christians ask us to pray with them, we should always take that opportunity. Something special happens when Christians pray together. We become closer to God and to one another.

"Brother" and "sister" become more than church words. What is more, when two or three agree in prayer, Jesus has promised to be with them.

Other Christians should be on our mind even when we pray alone. We have the privilege to pray for each other. Jesus prayed for his disciples and for us. Paul prayed for the churches. Prayer was never intended to be a selfish act. In prayer we intercede with God on behalf of our fellows. Their troubles become ours and then become his.

Praying with and for others also entails asking them to pray for us. Lone Ranger Christianity was never God's plan. When trouble comes we are not to grin and bear it. We are to pray and bear it. And we do not bear it alone; others help carry our burdens to God. Nothing would revitalize our churches more than a commitment to pray for one another and ask one another for prayer.

We Should Pray with the Entire Church

There is a place for public prayer. Through the centuries whenever Christians have met together for worship they invariably pray. Liturgical prayers have gained a bad reputation. In churches with written prayers there is the danger of insincerely doing things by rote. Christ condemns vain repetitions. In churches with spontaneous prayers, there is danger of thoughtlessness, flippancy, and performance. Praying to be seen is also condemned.

In short, public prayer in church is difficult. For the prayer leader there is pressure to say the right thing, to include all in the prayer, and to avoid praying to please people, not God. For the congregation there is the struggle to listen and to make the prayer our own. We must be able to say, "Amen."

God wills the church to pray together. When the whole church prays we experience the unity for which Christ prayed, "That they all may be one." In prayer we unite with one another and with the Father, Son, and Spirit.

We Should Cultivate a Habit of Prayer

Habit is a bad word. We usually speak only of bad habits, not good. "A habit of prayer" sounds like a contradiction. Is not prayer to be sincere, spontaneous, and heartfelt? If merely a habit, will it not lose its meaning?

Jesus had a habit of prayer. His prayers certainly did not lose their meaning. The early Christians were devoted to prayer. Paul prayed constantly. Doing something regularly, even habitually, does not necessarily make it boring and meaningless.

How do we develop a habit of prayer? It takes discipline. It might mean setting aside certain times of the day when, no matter what we are doing, we stop and pray. It might mean sometimes writing out prayers. Whatever technique one uses, the important thing is to pray regularly and often.

We Should Pray in the Crises of Our Lives

Regular prayer is the mark of the disciple. We pray when it is convenient and when it is not. But there are times that especially call for prayer. When our faith is weak, when illness strikes, when a loved one passes, when death is near, in all the dark valleys of life, we are brought to our knees in prayer. It is proper and right to pray when in need. Some Christians mistakenly do not want to bother God with their problems. But he loves us. He wants to be bothered.

When we pray in crises, we do not always know what to pray for. The Spirit will help us. When we pray in pain, we don't know how God will answer. He may remove the problem, no matter how big it is; he has the power. He may strengthen us so we can stand the pain. He may point us to the ultimate answer of the resurrection. Whatever his answer, we believe we are heard and we know his grace is enough for us.

Prayer Is More Than Asking for Things

We have emphasized the power and love of the God who hears our prayers and gives us what we need. But prayer is a much richer experience than merely applying for a blessing. In the New Testament, prayer always begins with praise and thanksgiving to God. When we pray we focus not primarily on our needs and wants but on the holiness and grandeur of our God. He is the Almighty. He alone is God. He alone worthy of our praise.

This gracious God made us, sustains us, and saves us. It is sheer grace that we stand in his presence. No amount of work can repay him for his love. Our most righteous deeds are filthy rags. When we have done all we can we still are worthless servants. The one thing we can do is thank him. As Christians our entire lives say thank you to God. Every action praises him. Every prayer is prayed with thanksgiving.

Thanksgiving, requests, and intercessions are parts of our prayers. Prayer is also communication with God. In prayer we speak, but we also listen. In prayer we come to know God's will and we become one with that will. Prayer energizes our spiritual lives.

Prayer Is Part of a Total Relationship with God

God is no slave to do our bidding. Prayer is no hocus-pocus to make our wishes come true. God is not in our power, we are in his. That is why biblical prayer is dangerous prayer. We dare not come to God only when we feel like it. Our prayers should reflect the whole of our life of obedience.

God wants us to pray. He wants us to ask him for what we need. But he really wants *us*, not our prayers. He wants all of us. Prayer then is not the only time we show our spirituality. All of life is our prayer to God. Working, playing, praying, sleeping, studying, caring—all are prayers if done to his glory.

There are special times called prayer, times when alone or with our brothers and sisters we bow before our Father. Yet prayer should not be an interruption in our lives; it should flow from our faith and our acts of service. Prayer is not just a righteous act, it is the act of one made righteous by the blood of Christ.

Studying about Prayer Is Not the Same As Praying

We end with a warning. If praying opens us up to the disruptive and dangerous relationship with God, there is something even more dangerous. Now that we know what the Bible teaches on prayer, we dare not return to our old prayer life. Quoting Scriptures on prayer is not praying. Knowledge without action is vain. Faith without works is dead. If we really believe what the Bible says on prayer, only one course is open to us: we pray—pray more, pray longer, and pray differently. Our Father is there to hear us. Our Savior is there to pray with us. The Spirit is there to help us.

Let us pray.

Questions for Further Discussion _____

1. Does prayer work? Is it better to say God works when we pray?

2. If prayer becomes a habit, does it begin to lose its meaning?

3. Should we ever be reluctant to pray in a crisis? What does it say about us if that is the only time we pray?

4. What is the most life-changing thing you learned in this study of prayer?

5. What are some specific ways your prayer life has changed as a result of this study?

Detailed Outline of Contents

PART FIVE: Praying with Early Christians in Acts and the Letters